Pra

Diana Ng reveals the
tices that still currently helps millions of individuals rid worries
and calm their chattering minds.

—The Reverend Dr. Lauren Artress, author of
*Walking a Sacred Path and The Sacred Path Companion*

The City of Surrey is proud to be home to the first public labyrinth
in the Lower Mainland. Located in Surrey's Fleetwood Park, the
seven circuit pathway is a place of reflection where residents can
enjoy the benefits a labyrinth offers.

—Dianne Watts, mayor of Surrey (2005–14),
British Columbia, Canada

# Walking the Labyrinth

# WALKING THE LABYRINTH

*Your Path to Peace and Possibilities*

## Diana Ng

R.N., B.SC.N., M.A.

KaDa PUBLISHING

Book cover photo by Diana Ng
Book cover design by Ares Jun

**Library and Archives Canada Cataloguing in Publication**

Ng, Diana, author
    Walking the labyrinth : your path to peace and possibilities / Diana Ng, R.N., B.Sc.N., M.A.

Includes bibliographical references. Issued in print and electronic formats.

ISBN 978-0-9939379-0-3 (paperback).—ISBN 978-0-9939379-1-0 (pdf)

    1. Labyrinths. 2. Labyrinths—Psychological aspects. 3. Labyrinths—Design and construction. I. Title.

BL325.L3N54 2015          203'.7          C2015-902352-1
C2015-902353-X

Published in Canada by KaDa Publishing

Printed in Canada

First edition

*For my family, Edmond, Katrina, and Danyka*

# Contents

# Acknowledgements

I WOULD LIKE TO THANK THE FOLLOWING PEOPLE FOR THEIR contributions to this book:

- All the labyrinth enthusiasts who shared a story and were as excited as I was in creating this book

- Bill Piket for your questions and feedback about my writing

- Jeff Saward for your comments on the "Labyrinth through Time" chapter

# Introduction

*In the silence between your heartbeats*
*hides a summons. Do you hear it?*
— TERMA COLLECTIVE

I HEARD THE CALL TO BUILD A LABYRINTH IN 2006. WHEN the opportunity arose, I seized it. In August 2008, I completed building the *first* outdoor public labyrinth in the city of Surrey, a suburb of Metro Vancouver—a 42-foot-diameter Classical seven-circuit labyrinth. As far as I was aware, there was no other community structure like this locally, from West Vancouver all the way to Hope.

At the time, I knew of only one other labyrinth, which is painted on the floor of a church in downtown Vancouver. Now, a new labyrinth is built every one or two years in Metro Vancouver. As of February 2015, there are approximately 4,600 labyrinths in more than seventy-five countries worldwide.[1]

With the increased numbers and popularity of labyrinths, I am writing this book to answer questions such as, Why are we drawn

---

1   From the website World-Wide Labyrinth Locator at labyrinthlocator.com, created by Veriditas and the Labyrinth Society..

to labyrinths? What inspires us to walk them? And ultimately, what drives individuals to build them?

This book will answer these questions by blending the art and science of mindfulness and of walking meditation in a labyrinth. I will show you how walking labyrinths can help you find happiness and answers to your life's deeper questions.

I will use personal stories of transformation to illustrate the many benefits these gentle, yet powerful, tools offer. All accounts are true, although pseudonyms are used and identifiable characteristics are disguised to protect personal privacy. To maintain narrative authenticity, genders haven't changed, as males and females have divergent traits. These anecdotes came from labyrinth enthusiasts, colleagues, and "familiar" strangers, who trusted me enough to share their stories.

After the labyrinth opening, I received many interested emails and telephone calls. And when these people heard I was collecting stories for a book, they would inevitably want to meet for coffee. I have also collected a few stories from people who belonged to a North American listserv dedicated to conversations about labyrinths. Each person I conversed with has personally experienced a sense of calm, clarity, and many other benefits as a result of walking these circuitous paths.

I invite you to try a labyrinth—to explore, discover, and enjoy the effects that come about by walking one.

Chapter 1

# Stepping into the Labyrinth

## My Story

*Be careful what you water your dreams with. Water
them with worry and fear and you will produce weeds that
choke the life from your dream. Water them with optimism and
solutions and you will cultivate success. Always be on the
lookout for ways to turn a problem into an opportunity for success.
Always be on the lookout for ways to nurture your dream.*
— LAO TZU

THIS IS MY STORY ABOUT ENCOUNTERING THE LABYRINTH, which began a new chapter in my life. I had worked for fifteen years as a health-promotions nurse in an oppressive organization. Its leaders were unaware of the volume and kind of work that was carried out by their few health-care professionals, who were of the same ethnicity as the vast number of families rapidly migrating to the city. At the same time, the amalgamation of two organizations created added pressures and chaos, causing the pre-existing undercurrents of conflict and tension to erupt. The workplace culture quickly became explicitly hostile and passive-aggressive. I sought assistance with employee rights on several occasions, but was unsuccessful. When the executive director sent defamatory emails to me and yelled at me to leave, I was no longer able to tolerate the toxic environment. I quit my job.

I remember the executive director shouting, "Your kind of people," and thrusting her arm in the direction of the door, motioning for me to go. Her pancake hand, pale and flat, flip-flopped like a swatter about to squash a mosquito. Animosity like vapor seeped beneath her porcelain mask. Her blue eyes pierced the silence. Her perfect haircut, a blonde pageboy, framed her large square face. She sat with her back rigid behind the large gray desk, her unyielding body clenched upright and tall beneath her dark pinstripe suit.

Determined to refuse to live the role of a victim or the lesser person that this leader of our organization had decided I was, I had to create a new path for myself. To remain dignified, to move forward, and to build a bright future, I decided to embark on a dream from a distant past.

This dream, like a piece of precious sculpture placed on a bookshelf to be admired and remembered every now and then, had been put away to make space for life's many occurrences. With employment out of the way, the path to this aspiration was clear and propelled my decision to return to school for my master's degree.

In the summer of 2000, I embarked on the quest of graduate school. The many transitions experienced that year were vibrantly intense, like the summer solstice becoming the autumn equinox. I was a middle-aged woman with two teenage children, and overnight I became a full-time adult student creating a future full of possibilities. Any pivotal change in a person's life, whether external or self-imposed, is a spiritual experience in that the world one knows is no longer the same. A new meaning must be conceived to align our psychic world with our physical one. We alone are the masters of our own life story. After traveling far away from our ordinary everyday realm or to another distant place, to return "home," and for our own development, we must bring significance to our journey. We must give our odyssey meaning and tell our story.

In graduate school, I stumbled on the labyrinth when I happened to open an email invitation to a labyrinth walk. At the time, not knowing what a labyrinth was, I thought this outdoor evening event seemed a satisfying way to end a hard day's work. I had little idea that my first labyrinth walk, a serendipitous event, would become a calling and begin my life's work to live more consciously and spiritually.

That evening my classmate Jennifer drew with white chalk an over-40-foot-diameter Chartres labyrinth on the asphalt of an empty parking lot, located on top of a plateau that overlooked the ocean. The reddish, setting sun gradually became a glowing line blurring the ocean and open sky. What seemed like hundreds of tea lights outlined the outside of this large labyrinth. Our community of fifty or more adult learners gathered around. With little explanation of what the walk was about, one by one, we entered and walked its winding path.

The activity was luminous and enlightening with tiny flames flickering in the gentle breeze. Taking one step at a time, I witnessed the vast gray ocean and infinite night sky become one. I felt joyous and free under the watchful moon and stars. The universe was light and tranquil; its largeness drew close, covering me like a thin sheet on a warm summer evening.

Stillness rested in my soul, aware and alert, calm and wondrous, yet all-knowing. There were no questions to entertain, decisions to make, or conflicts to navigate. Phenomenal presence—beauty, contentment, and fullness—filled me. An entire day of prolonged thinking had made my head tense, and I felt top-heavy, ready to fall over. The uneasy feelings of being a mature student, learning new concepts, and living in an unfamiliar environment vanished into the air. Peace wrapped its arms around me, as items fell off the to-do list in my head, lightening my body and soul.

I was amazed at the body movements of the other walkers. Some walked with such seriousness that each footstep was slow and precise, as if each stride was taken with full intent and purpose. Several walked buoyantly like they were welcoming the discoveries they were about to receive. One danced blissfully along the bending pathway grateful for where she was in the moment. A small number sat in the center of the labyrinth, focused, like they were hoping for something. Most, like me, walked in silence, losing track of time, as we placed one foot in front of the other.

What a beautiful tool this labyrinth was! It brought harmony to a group of diverse people with various interests and backgrounds. The labyrinth became the footprint for our class as we pilgrimaged for the next two years together. It expanded and deepened the meaning of our time together and our studies.

Today, I have let go of the unpleasant feelings from the meeting with the executive director, for I learned more about who she is and who I am, as people. That unfortunate experience opened doors to the work I am doing now. Since leaving that organization, I have taught courses on communication, professionalism, and leadership in nursing schools and business schools. When I am not teaching in an academic institution, I work as a leadership consultant to expand openness, democracy, and collaboration in organizations. Whenever and wherever I can, I speak about the labyrinth and use it as a tool for mindfulness and use walking meditation to integrate the mind, body, and spirit. When I introduce the labyrinth to groups, I emphasize appreciating the journey rather than just the destination. I place significance on being rather than doing.

## My Introduction to the Labyrinth

*We shall not cease from exploration*
*And the end of all our exploring*
*Will be to arrive where we started*
*And know the place for the first time.*
— T. S. ELIOT

In 2004, when I heard a woman was coming to Vancouver to teach others how to facilitate labyrinth walks as part of a conference, I knew I had to attend. I did have reservations when I found out that the presenter was a reverend from the Anglican Church; with a limited Christian background, I was hesitant about a biblical perspective on the labyrinth. However, I wanted to learn more about labyrinths, their spiritual applications for individuals and groups, and its community-building aspects in contemporary society. I was especially interested to hear others' experiences in their work with labyrinths. Since the conference was extraordinarily expensive, I decided that if I could find the money, I would go. If funds weren't available, I wouldn't go. It was a simple decision.

I submitted a grant proposal for this seminar to my *new* employer. Synchronicity was at work when, surprisingly, my application was approved. I knew I was taking a chance with this request, as I did not expect any employer to consider labyrinths as an innovative approach to teaching and learning. This was more than ten years ago, at a time when the word *spirituality* was barely whispered, let alone spoken in public. I thought it was a sign that employers were beginning to seek progressive leadership methods—perhaps an egalitarian, respectful, and mutual way of involvement in organizations. From this experience, I gained courage and persistence to be open to possibilities. I gratefully accepted the funds and attended the conference.

The presenter Rev. Dr. Lauren Artress's use of poetry and metaphors in her labyrinth presentation evoked in her audience an open heart and mind about being in touch with messages in our body. Her passion for sharing her knowledge was clearly demonstrated in the ways she interacted with the participants in the room. The participants came from diverse disciplines. I met a horticulturist, a musician/composer, an organizational development consultant, a grief counselor, a few church parishioners, and a Ph.D. student in adult education. The attendees and conference organizers were female, except for a lone male.

Since I was the single Asian person in the room and felt self-conscious, I had to accept that the spotlight shone bright on me each time I spoke. However, that did not stop me from maximizing my learning. Whenever I asked a question, the presenter grasped what I was asking and was most gracious in how she answered. I didn't gain all the knowledge I wanted during this one-and-a-half-day workshop, but I did develop a greater appreciation of the significance of labyrinths.

It was during this conference that I became excited and inquisitive about this increasingly popular, yet simple, symbol. I discovered that the labyrinth is a purposeful circular path and symbolizes wholeness and unity, change and growth. I was drawn to how labyrinths are powerful tools for reflection, discernment, and self-discovery. I wanted to comprehend how walking labyrinths reduces stress, quiets the mind, and provides insightfulness. This provoked me to dig deeper into the labyrinth's transformational abilities.

## How to Build a Public Labyrinth

*I find the great thing in this world is not so much where we stand as in what direction we are moving: To reach the port of heaven, we must sail sometimes with the wind and sometimes against it—but we must sail, and not drift, nor lie at anchor.*
— OLIVER WENDELL HOLMES

I was bubbling with excitement when I told a fellow member at church about what I had learned from Rev. Artress's conference. Without hesitation, we decided we had to build a labyrinth at the back of the seniors' center where we meet on Sundays. We had the idea that each member of our congregation would purchase one standard-size red brick (2¼ by 7½ by 3½ inches). A group of us would hand-dig a path for the bricks to form a Classical seven-circuit labyrinth.

To continue with this project, we had to get permission from the City of Surrey. But because a statue dedicated to veterans was at the same location, we didn't get it.

The city representatives suggested Hazelnut Meadows Park, a hilly but well-treed and quiet location near a train route. Its seclusion offered privacy for inner work in a public space—at least when the trains were not traveling past. A colleague and I visited the park and its nearby neighborhood. We decided on a spacious grassy area in a grove of young trees for a labyrinth.

Once we communicated our preference to the city folks, they offered yet again an alternate park, this time without any explanation. I was surprised; however, I did not question their decision and went with the flow. This time they suggested Unwin Park.

Unwin Park is an extensive recreational grassy park, housing an outdoor swimming pool with a well-equipped children's playground and a sizable parking lot. The relatively flat terrain made it easier to choose a site for the labyrinth. I saw that the park could make solitude challenging because of its wide open spaces with few trees, but I chose to view the merits, not the detractors, in both locations, as I wanted a labyrinth built in case the civic people changed their minds.

Knowing that this was to be the first public labyrinth in Metro Vancouver, I understood that—as with any new idea or innovation—resistance could be expected. It would entail massive education before the concepts of labyrinths were accepted and internalized by our community, society, and the world. I knew that I had to be courageously patient, if I was to be successful in this novel project.

Again, when we chose a site for the labyrinth at Unwin Park, I was referred to Fleetwood Park with little explanation. With bated breath, I continued with the process of visiting the new park, assessing its characteristics, and meeting its operational manager. During this period, I chose to stay positive, with the confidence that these city men wanted this labyrinth as much as I did, and I refused to entertain the thought the project could come to an abrupt end.

Fleetwood Park is located in a newer subdivision. This abundant acreage included a 1.8-kilometer forested hiking trail, a meandering creek with fish and wildlife, tennis courts, a well-equipped children's playground, and plenty of parking stalls. All these features were spaced far apart, maintaining the park's natural surroundings. I knew that I had found the perfect park for the labyrinth when I met the park's operations manager, who was as eager and enthusiastic as I was to have this addition to Fleetwood Park.

The park manager had a soft voice and was easy to converse with. He told me a bit about his family. The man and his family had traveled to walk labyrinths all over North America and Europe! He was an astute observer of the materials, styles, and sizes of labyrinths. As Rumi states, "Words are a pretext. It is the inner bond that draws one person to another, not words."

The city parks people and I signed an agreement that they would match each dollar I raised. They also offered a tax receipt for donations. I began to ask for contributions from various members of our congregation; however, it quickly became evident that there were not enough potential donors in our small church family. Although for many years I had attended a radically inclusive church that pioneered same-sex marriages, committed to environmental protection and offered liberal world religion and social-justice educational programs, I discovered we had several opposing attitudes and beliefs. Not every member bought into the values that a labyrinth offers. A small number of people were indifferent to this project, and some were skeptical or even overtly discouraging. A few told me outright that I would be unsuccessful in this venture. However, today, I continue to be appreciative of the ideas I learned and the people I befriended there. It's where I learned to have greater curiosity, to question, to explore what makes life meaningful. I learned the search is just as important as the answers; sometimes the search is even more significant.

Now fully committed to building this labyrinth, I had to try other avenues to obtain funding. I decided to approach the business community, since I was already networking to build my consultancy business. At that time, most of the business owners who came to networking events were men, with a handful of women. Though they listened politely whenever I told them about the progress of the labyrinth project, I knew on some level they thought I was foolish and wasting my time with an idea that would never succeed.

However, I continued to put on business fairs, where vendors paid a fee to showcase their products and services. I organized lotteries offering prizes. Money collected from the lotteries was added to the donations. I persistently asked for financial support from neighbors, friends, and family. These small sums eventually added up to a healthy amount.

Along the way, the project started to attract valuable media attention. I was interviewed by local newspapers and television and radio stations, such as the *Leader*, *The Now*, Joytv, and CBC radio. *Chatelaine* and *Alive* magazine, *Nursing BC* journal, the Surrey Board of Trade, and others requested interviews. Because of the increasing media attention I received, the city decided to bring the project to completion.

People from Surrey Parks and Recreation became approachable and open to suggestions I put forth for the labyrinth, such as the size, design, and construction materials.

Initially, we had conversations about which style of labyrinth would be appropriate—the Chartres or the Classical. The city wanted a Chartres, but I wanted a Classical. The Classical is the oldest type, remnants of it having been found in cultures all over the world. It would be the ideal style for our city, with its diverse population. After some hesitation, they agreed.

A construction company with a low bid was chosen through a competitive procedure. After a lengthy two-year process the labyrinth was finally complete.

The opening ceremony was held on August 28, 2008. Members of Surrey City Council, along with parks and recreation management and staff, came to support the ceremonial ribbon cutting and inaugural walk. Altogether, about thirty people including donors, family, friends, colleagues, and neighbors came to celebrate. South Fraser Unitarian Congregation provided tea, coffee, and sweets for the festive occasion.

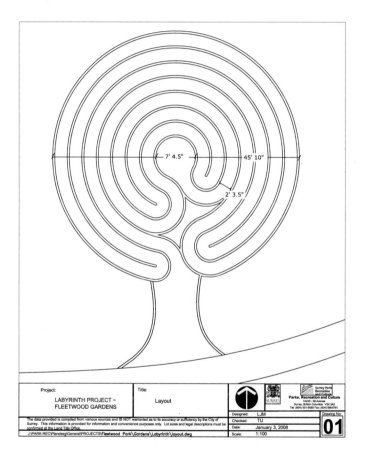

Labyrinth plan drawing for
Fleetwood Gardens in Surrey, BC.
Courtesy of City of Surrey.

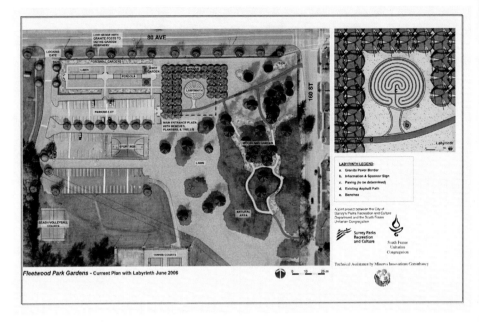

Site plan for labyrinth in Fleetwood Gardens.
Courtesy City of Surrey.

The Classical seven-circuit labyrinth is located on the north-east corner of Fleetwood Park, at 80th Avenue and 160th Street in Surrey, British Columbia. Surrey is a highly diverse multicultural city, with a population of about five hundred thousand people, and is approximately a forty-five-minute drive southeast of Vancouver.

With winding arms reaching 42 feet in diameter, the labyrinth silently waits to embrace everyone who enters. This winding path to peace is nestled in thick grass and surrounded by picturesque ruby maples, jade cedar hedges, and Celtic knot gardens. Dozens of colorful perennials and evergreen shrubs are located in two of its corners. As the three rows of maple trees become full and mature, they will be pruned to form a canopy enhancing solitude and peace for inner work. The tree canopy will form an umbrella, which will eventually keep a person dry from rain for at least

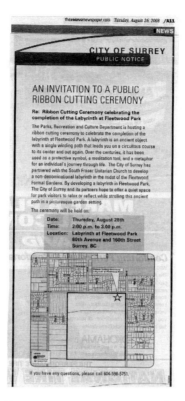

Newspaper announcement
on the opening of Metro Vancouver's
first outdoor public labyrinth.
Courtesy of the *Now* newspaper.

fifteen minutes. The walk on this path to calmness is about a quar-
ter mile, which is a gift for everyone in this fast-paced growing city.

The path for walking meditation is constructed of crushed
gravel, with attractive 4- by 4-inch reddish unpolished-granite
pavers for borders. The 7-foot-and-9-inch-diameter is eye-catching
and can comfortably accommodate several people simultaneously.
The labyrinth welcomes all, including the eclectic spiritualist
and religious devout like Serena. Serena, a labyrinth believer and

Fleetwood Gardens located in Surrey,
British Columbia at 15802 – 80th Avenue.

a Facebook friend, tells me that she was born into the Catholic Church, spent many years in the Baha'i Faith (the Baha'i community has no interest in labyrinths), and then found her home with the Universal Unitarians. She is now a Wiccan who continues to follow the teachings of Jesus.

Young men and women—dressed in their finest—have stood in front of this twisting path for graduation photos. Couples have created their own wedding ceremonies using this circular symbol. Nonprofit organizations have used the labyrinth to bring awareness to their causes. Coaches, counselors, and therapists have walked with clients to help them access their intuition, open their hearts, and hear their own inner voices for personal and professional transformation.

Andrea, a doctor in alternative medicine, told me she uses the labyrinth to introduce meditation and self-work to clients with no previous experience in these areas. The labyrinth has helped her clients turn their attentions inward, to be aware of their own thoughts and feelings.

Trevor, a university instructor, shared that he has his theology students walk the labyrinth on the first day of class. This has been an effective community-building activity, particularly with international students from all over the world—from as far as Somalia, China, Korea, and Africa.

The University of Massachusetts has a labyrinth in their library for stress-relieving meditation.[2] The labyrinth enables students to take breaks and relax from doing work on computers for an extended period of time.

Another labyrinth devotee, a blog writer, draws a huge labyrinth on a beach in Vancouver on the shortest and longest days of the year. To recognize and celebrate the summer and winter solstices, he invites people from the community to walk the labyrinth.

A retired senior spent over ten years making wooden finger labyrinths and giving them away. He has gifted more than two thousand labyrinths in a variety sizes and patterns to various people and organizations.

In my work as a leadership consultant, I have used the labyrinth in many ways. In one instance, I conducted visioning exercises utilizing the labyrinth with new Canadians, who have to re-create themselves and find employment when their professional credentials are not accepted in Canada.

---

2   Daniel Maldonado, "Library labyrinth targets stress," Daily Collegian, April 17, 2014, www.dailycollegian.com/2014/04/17/library-labyrinth-targets-stress/

On another occasion, I integrated the labyrinth with content I created about mental well-being and self-care. I presented this to women with eating disorders, who cope with anxiety, emotional distress, and life stresses by the cyclical bingeing and purging of food or by not eating at all. These participants learned a new tool to be present and calm, and to still the mind.

The famous singer and actress Olivia Newton-John found great comfort in the labyrinth when her partner was tragically lost in

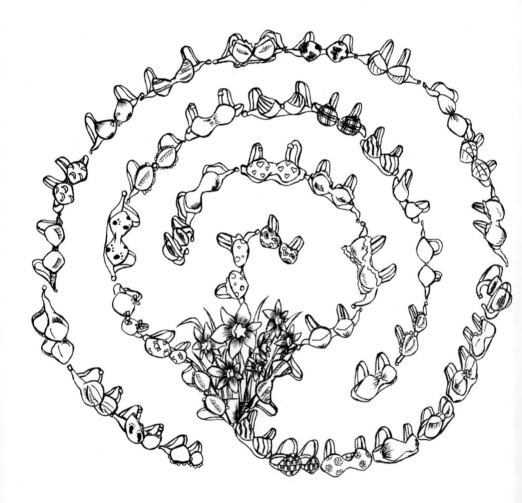

A labyrinth made with bras to
raise awareness for breast cancer.

a fishing trip and was never found.[3] Newton-John embraced the labyrinth again when she discovered the lump in her breast was cancerous.[4] She professed that she held onto daily grace and gratitude by walking her garden labyrinth.

3     Bill Hewitt, "Life after Loss," *People*, October 9, 2006, www.people.com/people/archive/article/0,,20060656,00.html.

4     www.olivianewton-john.com/NaturalHealthONJ.pdf.

A labyrinth created with shoes for footwear
donations and to raise funds for the homeless.

A food bank uses a labyrinth for canned and
boxed food donations and to raise funds.

# How to Build a School Labyrinth

*If every eight-year-old in the world is taught meditation, we*
*will eliminate violence from the world within one generation.*
— DALAI LAMA

In today's high-tech, fast-moving world, it is easy for children
and adolescents to become overstimulated. This is particularly so
when they race from one activity to another with technology constantly in hand. We, as parents adhering to a hectic schedule, act
as examples for our children.

We need to help children discover natural ways for the body and
mind to deal with the pressures of modern living and learn effective ways to remain focused on matters of importance. We need to
teach them the significance of staying in the present moment so
they can enjoy the good times while better managing the challenging ones.

Although research is in its infancy, literature demonstrates
that meditation improves attention, reduces stress, and improves
mood in children and adolescents. Mindfulness assists children
and adolescents to achieve greater concentration, increase focus,
and boost memory, which, in turn, sharpens learning.

On April 2, 2014, I was honored to spend the day building a
21-foot-diameter five-circuit Classical labyrinth for Forest Grove
Elementary School in Burnaby, British Columbia. The school has
a history of vandalism in recent years. Windows were smashed,
graffiti painted on its walls, a car set on fire in the playground, and
a portable toilet blown up. In an attempt to develop a community, where the children would take ownership and pride in their
school, an extensive vegetable garden was built and tended by
students. One year, they harvested enough produce to provide for

school lunches. The vegetable garden sparked an increased awareness of conservation and protection of the environment. A labyrinth would encourage the school's attitude for community and love for people and earth.

Lorraine, the project leader, was the one who invited me to participate in building the labyrinth. She is the mother of two children attending the school. Lorraine had learned about labyrinths from an older friend, who was very spiritual but not religious, and walked labyrinths on a regular basis.

Two years of hard work led up to the day's labor of measuring, drawing, digging, and building the actual labyrinth. Tireless months were spent speaking, meeting, and coordinating with various parent leaders, teaching and administrative staff, and grant providers to persuade them about the benefits of a labyrinth on the school grounds.

Despite the increasing popularity of labyrinths, the majority of people are unaware of labyrinths, nor do they understand their value. People tend to view the labyrinth solely on its physical form. They do not appreciate its intangible benefits. For Forest Grove Elementary, the labyrinth not only introduced the love for our land, earth, and world, it instilled pride in the school.

Lorraine wanted a teaching/learning, healing, and spiritual tool that everyone could use. In particular, she hoped the labyrinth would assist children to:

- Be open-minded

- Resolve conflicts

- Heal and make peace with trauma

- Learn meditation

- Ground restless energy

Approximately one hundred Grade 4 to Grade 7 students, their teachers, and volunteer moms came out on a nippy, early spring day. Surrounded by lush green trees and the lulling sounds of rustling foliage, enthusiastic participants hand-built the borders of the labyrinth with gravel and planted grass seeds in its pathways. Local hardy wildflower seeds were spread, so that in a few months the labyrinth would be encircled by bright, colorful blossoms.

From this project, the children learned, applied, and experienced lessons about not just diameters, circumferences, measurements, and volume, but also meditation, teamwork, and peace.

After the construction of the labyrinth was completed, the excited children lined up to walk its path. Following the walk, Lorraine shared a story about a student named Riana, and her experience while in the labyrinth. She spoke about Riana walking the winding path, when memories of her long-deceased family members filled the corners of her mind. Riana then saw images of an owl and an eagle. The student realized they represented her family, and that they would always watch over her. It was okay to let go of her dead brother and mother.

By building the labyrinth, the students witnessed and manifested creation, from concept to physical object. Students gained more than can be seen by our eyes.

This is the very first school in Metro Vancouver with a labyrinth on-site.

Photo of children building a school labyrinth.

# How to Draw a Labyrinth

This is a seed pattern for drawing a Classical seven-circuit labyrinth. Draw a labyrinth by simply following the arrow and connecting the lines and dots.

Chapter 2

# Labyrinths through Time

*The only thing that is constant is change.*

— Heraclitus

## The Greek Monster Myth

The word *labyrinth* is associated most often with Greek mythology; however, documentation of the actual term appeared in literature during early Christianity about 762 BC.[5] Widespread recognition of Christianity around AD 325 allowed the labyrinth symbol to be absorbed into later Christian symbolism, philosophy, and architecture, despite its pre-Christian origins.[6]

In the famous Greek myth, the sea god Poseidon gives a white bull to King Minos so that he can use it as a sacrifice. Minos decides to keep the bull instead. In anger, Poseidon makes the king's wife Pasiphae lust for and mate with the bull. Out of this

---

5    Homer, *The Iliad* and *The Odyssey*, undated; and Joel N. Shurkin and Inside
     Science News Service, "Geneticists Estimate Publication Date of *The Iliad*,"
     *Scientific American*, February 27, 2013, www.scientificamerican.com/article/
     geneticists-estimate-publication-date-of-the-illiad/.

6    Jeff Saward, "The Labyrinth in Ireland," *Labyrinthos*, February 2009, www.
     labyrinthos.net/irelandlabs.

union, an ugly monster called the Minotaur, which is part-bull and part-human, is born.

Daedalus, a skillful craftsman and artist, is summoned to build an elaborate container to hold this beast. When he finishes, Daedalus names the complex winding construction a *labyrinth*.

One day, King Minos's son is killed by Athenians. The angry king demands fourteen young Athenian men and women be sacrificed to the Minotaur every seven to nine years as reparation. Minos puts Ariadne, his young daughter, in charge of these offerings.

While organizing the ritual killings one day, the princess falls in love at first sight with the strong, handsome Theseus; he is standing tall among others as food for the Minotaur. Love spurs Ariadne to give Theseus a sword to slay the monster and a ball of thread to find his way out of the labyrinth. After Theseus achieves his goal, Ariadne elopes with Theseus aboard his ship to a faraway land. However, the story does not end there, as they do not live happily ever after. One day, Theseus abandons Ariadne and leaves the island, moving on to new adventures.[7]

## Christian Pilgrims

In her book *Walking a Sacred Path*, the Reverend Dr. Lauren Artress discussed the significance of labyrinths for Christians during a time when it was unsafe for them to travel to Jerusalem.[8] During the last decade of the twelfth century, these medieval pilgrims went instead to pilgrimage sites in northern France. Often, the end of their journey was a labyrinth made of stone and laid in the

7    Anne G. Ward, ed., *The Quest for Theseus* (London: Pall Mall Press, 1970).

8    Lauren Artress, *Walking a Sacred Path: Rediscovering the Labyrinth as a Spiritual Practice* (New York: Riverhead Books, 1995).

floor of the nave of one of the great Gothic cathedrals. The center of the labyrinths probably represented the Holy City itself for many pilgrims, and thus became the substitute goal of the journey.

The best-known labyrinth for this purpose is the beautifully preserved Chartres cathedral in France. No one actually knows when the labyrinth was constructed, because no surviving documents record that information. However, the architectural detective John James suggests the labyrinth must have been laid early in the first decade of the thirteenth century (circa 1201 to 1205 is a commonly quoted figure).[9] Craig Wright places its construction around 1215 to 1221 when the construction of the nave on the church floor was completed.[10] Today, the ancient Chartres labyrinth remains a favorite pilgrimage for modern seekers.[11]

## The Asian War Legend

In the seventeenth century, the Vatican sent a large number of missionaries to Nepal and Tibet. Over a period of about seventy years, missionaries traveled from India to these remote Himalayan countries.[12] Numerous reports and letters left behind by these religious people give unique information about these countries

9   John James, *The Master Masons of Chartres* (Leura, NSW, Australia: West Grinstead, 1990).

10  Craig Wright, *The Maze and the Warrior* (Cambridge, MA & London, UK: Harvard University Press, 2001).

11  Jeff Saward, "The Chartres Cathedral Labyrinth: FAQ's," Labyrinthos, August 2009, www.labyrinthos.net/chartresfaq.html.

12  Luciano Petech, *Il Nuovo Ramusio*, vol. 2, *I missionari Italiani nel Tibet e nel Nepal,I cappuccini Marchigiani* (Rome: 1952–53), cited in Staffan Lundén, "A Nepalese Labyrinth," reprinted in *Labyrinthos*, www.labyrinthos.net/nepalese.html.

during that time period. Father Cassiano da Macerata wrote about ancient ruins among giant, dense, old trees deep in the jungle, where wild, ferocious tigers, elephants, and rhinoceroses roamed. He described the Scimangada, an ancient burg with tall, thick fortress walls forming a labyrinth. The plan for this city can be found written in stone in the royal palace of Batgao in Nepal. (Today, the name for this regal Nepalese residency is Bhaktapur or Bhadgaon.)

Cassiano discovered a dramatic legend within the sustaining enclosure of Scimangada. Enormous fields suitable for agriculture and copious streams with fresh water produced sufficient food to feed the large population. Governed by a great king, with the assistance of prime ministers, it was a flourishing, peaceful compound.

One day, when the king openly disapproved of an official, the officer vowed vengeance. He allied with a Muslim emperor, and the officer and his troops destroyed defensive walls and entered the city before being noticed. They massacred the inhabitants. The officer successfully betrayed his fatherland and surrendered the complex to the Muslim emperor.

Several natives escaped the brutal ambush by running through a breach in the wall made by the enemies. One of these fugitives was a son of the king. This prince escaped to Nepal, where he eventually settled, built a followership, and seized the kingdom to become the king of the Nepalese people.

This myth, like all others, is partially written, partly passed down from previous generations in the form of an unforgettable epic. According to Nepali sources, Scimangada is also known as Simraongarh, Simaramapura, or Simraon. In 1097, it was founded as the capital city of Mithila by people from Karnataka. In 1325, Mithila was destroyed by the Muslims. The ruins of the city are still quite extensive, as seen by Cassiano. Today, Mithila is named Tirhut.

We know that there are fewer labyrinths in Asia compared to Europe. However, these winding paths have been found in the western and southern parts of India, leading to Sri Lanka.

Jeff Saward has detailed publications on his website about ancient labyrinths located in India and spreading as far as Java and Sumatra in Indonesia and southern Africa.[13] Although the origins remain mysterious, we know that they are at least four thousand years old. There is evidence that missionaries and foreign trade, during their lengthy stay, influenced the people in Nepal, Tibet, India, and as far as South Africa to incorporate these circuitous paths into their lives. Saward's website lists labyrinths found worldwide in Brazil, Arizona, Iceland, and across Europe.

## A Scandinavian Blessing

Over three hundred stone labyrinths still exist in Scandinavia.[14] Some are found near burial grounds and execution sites suggesting involvement in death rituals. However, many are often located by shorelines. Seaside people believed these Scandinavian stone pathways could tame dangerous winds and storms. Ocean-going men would walk a labyrinth seven times to rid themselves of evil spirits prior to heading out to sea. They would wind to the center of the labyrinth and run out as quickly as possible. Seafaring men believed their fast exits would escape trolls, gremlins, or other menaces. Once caught in the center of the labyrinth, the spirits were trapped.

Fishermen walk them even today for the blessing of a good daily catch, a favorable wind, and a safe return home.

13     Lundén, "Nepalese Labyrinth."

14     John Kraft, *The Goddess in the Labyrinth* (Turku, Finland: Åbo, 1985).

# Modern Significance

The ancient labyrinth found in Nepal, unlike the European ones, was used for military purposes. The town was incorporated into the winding paths of the colossal labyrinth and protected a substantial, sustainable farming community. The gigantic winding paths stood as a bulwark against intruders.

The Greek description of the labyrinth is that of complicated paths, a trap that, once entered, negates hope that one can ever return to the outside world. It is a contraption designed to disempower and to restrict freedom.

The word *labyrinth* has been used synonymously with *maze* in the English-speaking world over the centuries. These multicursal paths, like puzzles to be solved, are full of dead ends and blind alleys intended to bewilder, frustrate, and make you lose your way. The maze is a left-brain task that requires logical, sequential, analytical activity to find the correct path into the maze and out. Choices are a constant in these complicated passages. In North America, mazes are typically found in entertainment parks and tourist attractions.

There is common agreement among experts, researchers, and enthusiasts that today labyrinths are used as a metaphor for the journey of life. (Compare this with the uses of legendary ancient labyrinths.) They are a tool, a process that is more significant than the structure itself. Labyrinths are like helpers accompanying us to find answers and live peacefully, when there is no road map in the mysteries of life. In the labyrinth, we are more likely to become aware of our emotions and thoughts particularly during adverse situations. The website for the organization Veriditas (veriditas.org) describes a labyrinth as "a walking meditation, a path of prayer, a crucible of change, a watering hole for the spirit, and a mirror of the soul."

As well, it is now generally accepted that labyrinths have one pathway that twists and turns from the entrance or mouth to the goal—or center—which symbolizes our deepest self. From the center, the path winds outward, out of the circle, which brings the walker to a broader understanding of who she or he is as a person. It is a right-brain activity involving intuition, creativity, and heart. A labyrinth is an archetype for meditation, reflection, and contemplation. We can walk it. The direct experience offers something about ourselves waiting to be discovered.

With a labyrinth, there is one choice to be made. The choice is to enter or not—to walk a path of spirit. A passive, receptive mindset is needed. A quiet, still mind is needed for our inner voice to appear. That inner consciousness guides our actions and behaviors.

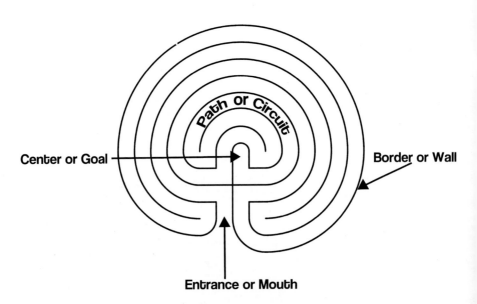

This drawing shows the parts of a labyrinth.

The Classical seven-circuit labyrinth in this example shows that you enter a labyrinth through the mouth and then walk on the paths or circuits. The walls keep you on the path. The goal is the center of the labyrinth. When you reach it, you have gone half the distance—you now need to turn around and walk back out.

In the last decade, North Americans have rediscovered the labyrinth as a tool for mindfulness and well-being. Labyrinths have been installed in hospitals, schools, churches, retreats, wellness centers, and funeral homes. There are individuals who have made a tremendous effort to build one on their property. A female contestant requested a labyrinth to be built in her backyard when she was chosen as the winner for a home-renovation television show.[15]

. . .

Abbey is a fellow labyrinth enthusiast in that we have much in common and are both on a spiritual journey in our work with labyrinths. She, a horticulturist, and her husband, an engineer, designed and built an enormous, permanent outdoor labyrinth on their private seven-acre rural property in Langley, British Columbia. The almost round Classical labyrinth created with over 550 plants is 125.5 feet long by 116 feet wide. Its two-foot-wide borders are made of raised garden beds of mainly yews, cedars, alders, viburnums, potentillas, blueberries, and pansies. Its center, measuring 44.5 feet long by 26 feet wide, is a grass sphere with an oak tree surrounded by lavender, pansies, and woolly thyme. Bark mulch forms the four-foot-wide walking paths, which are a half-kilometer to the center. Walking this entire labyrinth, designed to offer a deep sensory experience, takes approximately one hour.

15    See photos of the episode of *Leave It to Bryan* called "A Leak of Faith" at www. hgtv.ca/leaveittobryan/episodes (season 3, episode 16).

In the summer of 2012, when our old backyard patio was damaged, we built a new one with paving stones embedding a five-circuit labyrinth pattern. By walking this labyrinth on a regular basis, I was able to stay calm, focused, and productive while I wrote this book, sought the Surrey World Labyrinth proclamation, and built my business.

Our brick patio labyrinth.

Chapter 3

# The Harmony of
# Walking Meditation

*Walk and touch peace every moment.*
*Walk and touch happiness every moment.*
*Each step brings a fresh breeze.*
*Each step makes a flower bloom under our feet.*
—THICH NHAT HANH

WHEN I FIRST DECIDED THAT I WANTED TO LEARN MEDITATION, I signed up for a sitting-meditation class, as that was the one form of meditation I knew about. I had no idea how challenging it would be to learn this skill. Despite my best efforts, I soon gave up as I found it too irritating to still my restless body and mind. After sharing my experience with others, I discovered that a lot of beginners find learning to meditate a struggle.

It was hard for me watch other beginners like myself trying to learn this skill. Some found its physical demands too much for their bodies to handle. Rosemary was one such person. In her sixties, Rosemary signed up for meditation lessons as a way to gain more energy and vitality. However, she found it physically challenging to follow the teacher's instructions. Being forty pounds or so over-weight and slightly arthritic, it was painful for Rosemary to get down on the floor to sit in a cross-legged position for any length of time, and it was doubly difficult for her to get back up into a standing pose again. She would clumsily get on her hands and knees and roll herself into a cross-legged sitting position. Not too long after, she would awkwardly roll herself again onto all four hands and knees, to hoist her body into a standing position.

Rosemary is not alone. Like her, many people are unable to achieve sitting meditation. Some have tried lying down, though it can also be very difficult for them to get down onto the floor mat or find comfort lying down in such a way. What's more, it's not uncommon for people to fall asleep while meditating lying down, which can be a source of embarrassment (worse if you find out you may have snored).

Walking meditation is a wonderful alternative for people who would like to meditate but are unable to remain in the sitting or lying position, as well as for those find it difficult to stay still for more than a few minutes. Daniel, a young professional who works long hours, falls in the latter category. His mother shared with me that Daniel finds it hard to sit still and is constantly plugged into technology. Encouraged by his mother to practice calmness and stillness, he is open to the concepts of meditation; however, the thought of having to sit in silence for any length of time is excruciating for him.

Walking meditation would be beneficial for Daniel and others like him, who work extended hours at a sedentary job and find it hard to calm their minds in our hyperconnected Internet world.

For Myra, a retired patient-care nurse who suffers chronic lower back pain, discovering walking meditation has been a gift. As an experienced sitting meditator, walking meditation has allowed her to continue with this essential practice, as she is no longer able to sit for long.

Indeed, for people like Daniel and Myra, who spend considerable time sitting at work or who are unable to tolerate sitting, walking meditation can serve as a powerful bridge between meditation practice and daily life, helping them to be present, mindful, and concentrated in their ordinary activities. It can reconnect us to the simplicity of being and the wakefulness that comes from it.

The sensations of walking can be more compelling than the subtle sensations of breathing while sitting. In sitting meditation, one strategy is to focus on our breaths as we observe the thoughts in our mind. This is difficult for some people. It is my belief that people can find that they are more intensely and easily aware of their bodies while walking in meditation. Certainly, while dealing with strong emotions or stress, walking mediation may be more relaxing than sitting still.

After a meal, upon waking from sleep, and following a long period of sitting or sitting meditation, walking meditation can be quite helpful. An added benefit is that, when done for extended times, walking mediation can build strength and stamina.

For instance, sixty-five-year-old Matthew used the finger labyrinth in his recovery after his sudden stroke. In the early days after this serious illness, each hour, each day, and each week lasted interminably with no or little healing noted. The mood fluctuations, along with impatience, frustrations, and loss of productivity produced a turbulent convalescence.

Labyrinth boards allowed him to trace a labyrinthine path on a small surface with his fingertip, which helped to clear and calm the mind. These exercises afforded Matthew to manage and shift the negative emotions and thoughts that came with this serious illness. Despite the negative emotions of fear and sorrow, circling the small, warm wood-grained tabletop labyrinth with his finger shifted these feelings. It was like an affirmation, reminding him to stay undisturbed and work patiently with his situation rather than resist it.

As his health improved, he began to walk a floor labyrinth. Walking meditation can be part of an intervention to rebuild the health of the mind, body, and spirit. Matthew gauged his convalescence by the number of circuits and times he could walk the labyrinth.

Certainly, as in Matthew's experience, walking meditation can take the form of walking the paths of a labyrinth, which can be especially healing and relaxing. Walking the labyrinth keeps the mind focused on the route and on the act of walking. It is much easier to let the mind wander, when moving along an undesignated course as compared to following a pathway within a labyrinth.

Regardless of where we walk, the mechanics of moving our legs, the largest muscles in our body, promotes the discharge of pent-up energies—especially the negative ones. Feelings, particularly those that come with the mundane aspects of daily living, are repressed and stored in our body. Walking meditation in the labyrinth is a healthy and effective method to release these unhealthy emotions.

I have been asked whether it is the unhealthy emotions or repression of these emotions that is unhealthy. We know that there is a strong link between the body, mind, and spirit.

Gail, a young woman, enjoys walking outdoors in the sunshine. Mesmerized by the beauty of the blue irises, pink peonies, and salmon poppies, she walks with lightness in her posture and her arms and legs freely sway back and forth. When she suddenly sees what she believes is a three-foot-long brown snake on the dirt road, she screams, tenses all the muscles in her body, and runs as fast as she can. Ten feet away, she stops, gasps for air, and looks back for a better look at the snake. Once she notices that the thing is rigid and motionless on the ground, she quickly realizes that the "snake" is a tree branch. Giggling to herself and feeling foolish, Gail relaxes and returns to her delightful carefree strides again.

This anecdote illustrates the body, mind, and spirit connection in that there is no separation between our physical bodies, our thoughts, and our emotions. This holds true for both positive as well as negative emotions. Negative emotions such as prolonged, unmanaged sadness, loneliness, and severe anxiety can lead to depression. People with a mild form of depression have low energy, are not as interested in social activities, and experience altered sleep and diet patterns.

The deteriorating effect of negative thoughts causes negative emotions, which in turn results in negative physiological responses. Walking meditation helps us to become aware of our thoughts, release negative emotions, and delay or obstruct the undesirable physiological reaction. Meditating with our feet in motion assists us to become aware of what is happening in our body, including our thoughts and emotions. This powerful body-mind-spirit con- nection supports us in choosing the right actions toward health and well-being. No wonder the Vietnamese Buddhist monk Thich Nhat Hanh suggests that we carry out walking meditation with a half-smile.[16]

Meandering the circuits of the labyrinth can produce a deep state of relaxation and a tranquil mind. Today meditation is con- sidered a type of complementary mind-body medicine, and is commonly used for relaxation and stress reduction. After an over- whelming and stressful day of work or after spending long hours

16    Thich Nhat Hanh, *The Miracle of Mindfulness: An Introduction to the Practice of Meditation* (Boston, Beacon Press: 1996).

in the company by whom I feel judged or criticized, which, in turn, causes me to be cautious of what I say and how I behave, I turn to walking the labyrinth as the easiest way to let go of these mental defilements that have built up. I walk the twisting paths of the labyrinth to be centered and to release the adverse energies that have accumulated and continue to be harbored in the body without any useful purpose.

Sometime ago, I was going through a stressful legal process. I was defending myself against an unscrupulous lawyer, whose desire was to win at all costs. The thunderous man wore his belt tight around his protruding abdomen giving his body the shape of a large sausage with a tourniquet in the middle. Gray hair topped his balding scalp and distorted face. He had a loud and abrupt voice like a jackhammer on cement. It was doubly difficult to observe the two female assistants, who danced around this mean and arrogant man, loyally serving without questions, as if his thoughts were the ones that counted, the right ones.

After each of the unpleasant days during the legal process, I would walk the labyrinth to clear away the ugly images that remained in my mind. Its winding paths helped me to focus on the present, to accept and let go of the difficult experiences, to receive new insight, and to appreciate all the wonderful people in my life.

I continue to walk this winding path as a way to self-awareness. To remain calm—which enables clear thinking in stressful situations—is probably the most important reason why I continue to be committed to the practice of walking meditation in the labyrinth. Sometimes walking the labyrinth offers more than words can describe.

Come walk the labyrinth with me as a way to gain the energy we need to do the work we are meant to do and be joyful in a world that focuses far too much on domination rather than cooperation, on differences rather than similarities, on wrong rather than right, and on separation rather than togetherness. Come walk with me for harmony.

Chapter 4

# Life Purpose: A New Path for Modern Pilgrims

*To live is to risk dying.*

—Anonymous

THEY FOUND SARAH'S BODY ON ITS SIDE, COLD AND STIFF, on the reddish hardwood floor. My friend had been dead for two days. I would have thought this was the cruelest of gossip had I not been told this horrific news by her ex-husband. My stomach felt heavy and churned like rocks spinning in a small centrifuge. Dark, clammy chills spread through my body when I thought about what had happened to her.

Images of her dressed in vivid-colored flower-pattern dresses coordinated with bold jewelry raced through my mind, her artistically painted face of blue eye shadow, red rouge, and pink lipstick. They could not cover the sadness and pain that lingered far too long. A vibrant woman of a thousand untold stories, she loved to have people around her. Despite having many close family members and friends, her happiness had lasted for fleeting moments.

I think about her even more when I walk by her white house at the back of a long driveway. Today, the house feels like it is veiled by a shade of gray. The six magnolias she planted years ago along that path are now mature and in full bloom, lush with shades of beautiful white, pink, and purple flowers. They stare at me in silence as I pass by, stuck in time. If they could talk, I think the plants would be asking, "What do you see? What are you doing with your time?"

Spring is not a good time to die, if there is ever a right time to depart life. The endurance of the cold winter beneath damp, dreary skies is finally over. The impatience and frustration in the lengthy wait for the first appearance of snowdrops, those tiny white delicate elongated globes, has just ended.

No. Spring with its brilliant colors is about anticipation, beginnings, and celebrations. An ending in spring does not make sense, none at all. But then, when does the instant termination of life make sense? Do sudden losses have to make sense? Tell me—don't we all die in the end?

I vicariously met death again, touching intensely the fragility and unpredictability of life. Death comes suddenly without announcement. We don't know when we will die. We just know that all life ends, despite the lack of its acceptance in our modern, technologically advanced world. In my social circles, when someone dies, hours are spent talking about what caused death, the final physiological failure to sustain life. Don't tell me the reasons for the last breath? Rather, "Tell me how will you live knowing you will die?"

I invite you to walk the labyrinth to discover what possibilities await you.

# Guidelines to Walking a Floor or Ground Labyrinth

This section will shift the perception of labyrinth from mere building materials of granite pavers, gravel, and rocks to powerful internal processes for exploring, discovering, and cultivating our inner landscape—our mind, body, and spirit. Through regular practice of mindfulness and walking meditation on these circuitous paths, you will feel in charge of your random thoughts and feelings. You will feel empowered, respond positively in various situations, and deal with problems effectively.

The labyrinth, on the surface, is a well-defined circular path on the ground, which leads to a center. Sometimes, this center is an enlarged circle. When walkers arrive in the center, they turn around, following the identical path out.

There are several styles of labyrinths. The oldest known is the Classical seven-circuit labyrinth, also called the original labyrinth, dating back to four thousand years.[17] I favor this one above all others, as remnants of this original labyrinth have been found in cultures and countries all over the world. Hence, the Classical seven-circuit labyrinth represents diversity. Long ago, these stone labyrinths varied in size. Today, there are as many sizes and styles of labyrinths as there are people's unique creative expressions. People have made labyrinths out of the following:

17    Jeff Saward, "The First Labyrinths," *Labyrinthos*, 2007, www.labyrinthos.net/firstlabs.html.

| | | |
|---|---|---|
| Turf | Rope | Vinyl |
| Stones | Plants | Chicken feed |
| Bricks | Driftwood | Shoes |
| Sand | Paint and chalk | Canned food |
| Gravel | Lights | CDs |
| Concrete | Candles | Books |
| Glass | Cloth | Projectors |
| Lime | Canvas | Bras |

Regardless of its type and surface materials, the labyrinth has a deeper meaning. It is a metaphor for the journey of life. Our awareness of life is the pilgrimage. A walk in the labyrinth encourages us to experience the spiritual, and cultivate our awareness of feelings and intuition. In essence, we learn that life itself is a pilgrim's journey.

By entering the path, we intentionally leave our exterior world and travel its winding path to our interior landscape. By pacing one step at a time, we walk the circle to the labyrinth's center. Its center, for some, is a place of stillness where our small voice is heard. The center is symbolic of the heart and soul of who we are. Our essence, derived from our values and principles, awaits discovery and clarification while in the center of the labyrinth. A Facebook friend Marty puts it this way: "The center of the labyrinth is a mystery to be revealed. It is the turning point for one who has the desire to find and live our own principle." Ray, another Facebook friend, explains it like this: "All labyrinths are pathways within the Universal Circle leading us to our shared center, the

Center of All Hearts. But I don't think about this when I walk a labyrinth. I'm in experiential, intuitive mode when I reach the Center, and I typically experience a dynamic peace and stillness. I say *dynamic* because I experience the Center as alive and interactive—a sanctuary." The center represents the heart and soul of an individual, and the collective mankind.

The path out from the center represents leaving our inner world, sometimes with a gift; back to our outer world. The gift can be a sense of peace and joy, an insight, an answer, more energy, a focus, etc. . . . We can always count on the pathway taking us safely to the center, and we can always count on it taking us safely out again.

Over time, with disciplined practice, every step of a walking meditation is a way to keep mind and body together on the path. There is no destination but the here and now—neither running toward nor away from. Many people have discovered peace and happiness in walking meditation.

Join me in walking a floor or ground labyrinth for mindfulness meditation. Sometimes, an insight or an answer to a question may reveal itself as you move one foot slowly in front of the other along this winding path.

First, here are guidelines for walking floor or ground labyrinths:

1.  There is no right way or wrong way to walk a labyrinth.

2.  Walk with ease, at a comfortable pace.

3.  Be respectful of others when walking the labyrinth.

4.  Feel free to pass ahead of the people who are walking slower.

5. Meditative or relaxing music and/or candles may be used with the labyrinth walk. Sometimes this helps to engage the chattering thinking brain, thus turning our attention inward.

6. It may be helpful to keep your eyelids partially closed. This decreases stimulation from outside.

7. Take three deep breaths at the entrance: inhale deeply into the bottommost of your lungs and exhale each breath slowly and completely. The deep breaths help invite presence.

8. As you enter the path, be mindful of your feelings, your thoughts, and the sensations in your body. (Observe these thoughts like watching clouds drift by high up in the sky. Do not engage with the thoughts. By viewing them, the thoughts will fade, lose their intensity, and calm you.)

9. Focus on putting one foot in front of the other. Make the contact between your feet and the ground peaceful and serene. (Well-known Buddhist master Thich Nhat Hanh suggests that we walk as if we are kissing the earth with our feet.)[18]

10. Some like to walk barefoot so that they are touching the earth, or with socked feet if walking on a canvas labyrinth.

11. Be silent.

12. Enjoy the stillness. (We must be still to move into another state of consciousness.)

---

18   Thich Nhat Hanh, *The Long Road Turns to Joy: A Guide to Walking Meditation* (Delhi, India: Full Circle, 1996).

13. Again, be attentive to what is happening inside of you.

14. When you reach the center, the largest part of the pattern, stay there for as long as you like.

15. Leave the center when you feel you are ready.

16. Continue to be mindful of your feelings, thoughts, and sensations in your body, as you put one foot in front of the other on your journey back to the exterior world.

17. When I am at the end of the path, outside the labyrinth, I usually turn to face it and say "thank you" before moving onto other activities.

18. You can walk the labyrinth again or around its perimeter if you feel unsettled. (I sometimes walk the outside of the circular path both ways until I feel grounded.)

19. If you have time following your walk, journal alone in silence, without self-censorship. You may be pleasantly surprised to discover gems, wisdom, or insight in your writing.

20. Observe and reflect on your writing. What has come up for you? Does your writing inform you of what is happening in your life? What did you receive? An insight or inspiration? Do you need to make changes to your circumstances?

21. Daily practice is best; however, some people find this too arduous. If so, commit to a consistent schedule. Something wonderful will come up for you. An idea, an answer, a decision, a possibility of making peace with a situation, and an insight are all possible. The key is to make walking the labyrinth a *regular* practice.

The Reverend Dr. Lauren Artress explains the three general stages of walking a labyrinth in her book *Walking a Sacred Path*:[19]

- Releasing on the way in

- Receiving in the center

- Returning when you follow the return path

Symbolically, and sometimes in actuality, you take back into the world that which you have received. This may be tranquillity, an answer to a problem, or understanding an irritating experience.

## How to Use a Finger or Lap Labyrinth

If you do not have a ground or floor labyrinth nearby, you can use a finger, tabletop, or lap labyrinth. Sometimes they are called labyrinth boards as well. These are commonly made from wood, plastic, and clay. However, oftentimes people create their own finger labyrinths with beans, pebbles, and beads. I have seen labyrinths embroidered, collaged, and painted onto canvas. These finger labyrinths help people to quiet their minds, manage anxiety during transitions, and invoke creativity. Here are suggestions to support you in getting the most from your labyrinth board experience:

1.  Find a place where you can sit alone quietly. You may wish to choose a spot under a tree, an empty room, or a quiet corner.

2.  Play relaxing music or light a candle (options). This helps to engage the chattering brain, thus focusing our attention inward.

19    Lauren Artress, *Walking a Sacred Path: Rediscovering the Labyrinth as a Spiritual Practice* (New York: Riverhead Books, 1995).

3. Be comfortable. Sit upright with proper support for your back.

4. Place your finger on the mouth or entrance of your lap labyrinth.

5. Close or partially close your eyes.

6. Take three deep breaths to invite presence—the here and now.

7. Slowly move your finger along the grooves. (I have witnessed people barely moving their fingers to prolong the experience. Also, some people find that lifting their finger from the labyrinth disturbs the meditation process.)

8. When you arrive at the center, leave your finger there for as long as you like, as if you were just walked into the center of a ground labyrinth. When you are ready, leave the center, following the groove, symbolically returning to the outside world with what you have gained.

9. Again, move your finger slowly at the comfortable pace.

10. When I am at the end of the grooves, I say "thank you" to complete the experience.

11. You may do another labyrinth "walk" with your finger until you are centered.

12. If you have time following your finger walk, remain silent and alone and write without restraint. Your writing may astonish you with new revelations, understandings, and intuition.

13. Be mindful, reflect, and ponder on your writing. What are your observations? Does your writing inform you about your current life condition? What positive or negative pieces do you find? Meaning making will come in time.

14. A consistent practice is most beneficial. (See pages 44–46.)

Joan, an executive client, keeps a wooden finger labyrinth in her desk. She meditates with the labyrinth prior to entering a tense board meeting. This gives her the confidence to remain grounded and focused.

Another client Suzie, who is a working mother with two young children, meditates with her finger labyrinth three times a day to foster alertness and sanity despite her hectic schedule. She meditates immediately when she awakes in the morning to set intentions for the day. When she arrives home from work, she meditates to consciously switch roles from employee to mother. Before she goes to bed, she repeats the process to shed the day's angst and the whirling head talks. As a result, she sleeps better.

Also, Suzie prominently displays her beautiful 12½-inch-diameter wood-grain finger labyrinth on her credenza at work. Staff come by to admire this artistic piece. Sometimes, they trace its grooves with their fingers, circling back and forth, playing, losing track of time. Suzie continues to share that her wooden finger labyrinth invites warmth. She finds tranquillity by looking at it, like triggering a state of peace. This has facilitated her to be focused, productive, and calm in her workplace.

Suzie enjoys her wooden finger labyrinth so much that she takes it on vacation. She claims the labyrinth is now her religion, as finger walking her wooden labyrinth furthers her to make choices of higher power.

A news reporter expresses the same sentiment as Suzie in an article on the CNN *Belief Blog*. The journalist writes how the labyrinth alleviates her worries in raising and parenting her autistic son. It is encouraging to know the labyrinth strengthens people when they are faced with life's challenging demands.[20]

## How to Use a Labyrinth Drawn on Paper

If you do not have access to a ground or finger labyrinth, a final alternative is a paper labyrinth as shown on page 51. Follow the same instructions as for finger-walking a labyrinth (see pages 47–49). You may use the tip of your finger or a pencil for this.

I have heard women prisoners use the tips of pencils to meditate on labyrinths drawn on paper to quiet unwanted stories in their heads and find peace in prison living conditions over which they have little control. I am certain this activity is equally beneficial for male prisoners.

---

20    Sally Quinn, "My Faith: How Walking the Labyrinth Changed my Life," CNN *Belief Blog*, October 8, 2011, religion.blogs.cnn.com/2011/10/08/my-faith-how-walking-the-labyrinth-changed-my-life/

Chapter 5

# Mindfulness: Your Path to Peace and Possibilities

*The breeze at dawn has secrets to tell you.*
*Don't go back to sleep.*
— RUMI

MINDFULNESS IS CHALLENGING TO DEFINE OR DESCRIBE, for it has a distinctive meaning for each individual dependent on their level of awareness. It is an inherent quality of human consciousness that cannot be easily measured like 100 milliliters, 40 ounces, or 2 feet by 4 feet. It is a state that, with practice, can be developed and deepened to a higher order of consciousness. This condition of the mind becomes clearer and more effective as one purposely pays attention—nonjudgmentally—in the present moment.[21] It is an open and receptive awareness of what is occurring in the here and now. Through intentional attention in the moment, alertness arises in an open, accepting, and discerning way to whatever is occurring. The aim is to develop this acquired skill to a high degree to make it possible for a life with a vivid,

---

21 David S. Black, "A Brief Definition of Mindfulness," Mindfulness Research Guide (2011), www.mindfulexperience.org/resources/brief_definition.pdf.

clear mind every minute of the day, so that sensations, thoughts, emotions, and memories can be experienced as they truly are. With training, consciousness helps us to wake up from a life lived on autopilot, a life based on habitual responses. Mindfulness is a general receptivity and full engagement with the present moment. A person fully aware with this higher level of mental clarity differs from another, who is preoccupied with the past or worried about the future, which interferes with being fully in the now.

Walking the labyrinth is a tool for developing mindfulness in everyday life. Walking meditation in these circuitous paths leads to mindfulness, and keeps our consciousness alive and alert to reality. Decades ago, meditation and mindfulness were popular in religious circles exclusively, and its full potential attainable only by those involved in religious practices.

Meditation while walking is spiritual, profound, and meaningful to the walker. The process of walking engages our intuitive, pattern-seeking, symbolic mind from which creativity emerges. Buddhist monks have practiced walking meditation for thousands of years to deepen their understanding of the sacred and mystical forces of life.

Borrowed from the Buddhist tradition dating back thousands of years ago, walking meditation is the lesser known among the other three approaches: sitting, lying, and standing. North Americans are now taking notice of what the monks have enjoyed for so many years. The simplicity and ease of walking meditation in the labyrinth is changing these perceptions, and is gaining attention for its health and spiritual benefits.

What often hinders individuals from trying meditation is the challenge of overcoming the restlessness and discomfort of sitting quietly for an extended period of time. With consistent, regular practice over time, this skill can transform our day-to-day life into one of continuous meditation, and transform the mundane into the spiritual.

Buddha describes spiritual means to search and investigate the true nature of the mind. It begins with setting good intentions. When you are mindful, you are using your brain to live a life of well-being, create a healthy lifestyle, and minimize stress.

. . .

In the early 1990s, I became curious about sitting meditation. As a young career mother, I noticed the thoughts in my mind were running faster than my body. My agitated brain, constantly thinking about whether I had completely finished one task as I quickly moved to the next item on the to-do list, made fatigue easy and relaxation difficult. I actively sought remedies when I decided that I needed more patience to be a better parent and to manage existence better.

As I knew of only sitting meditation in Buddhism at the time, I explored this by attending classes in our community. I found it very difficult to sit still. I could not sit cross-legged in silence among others in the room, and before very long, thoughts became loud, racing fiercely and fast in circles, refusing to leave.

Sometimes I fell asleep in the lotus position, leaning against the wall for support. Each time I questioned the lemon-haired instructor about what was happening to me, he said, "Go home and go to sleep."

It was a dismal experience, as I don't think my mind was ever calm. It wavered between restlessness and sleep during those classes. Familiarity with the words *calm* and *peace* on an intellectual level did not produce the calm and peace experientially.

Walking meditation, on the other hand, and particularly in the labyrinth, offers a rhythmic structure that can enable those who struggle to stay focused during sitting meditation to attain concentration. The labyrinth walk further enhances the meditative experience, because a specified path is laid out, allowing the person to fully focus on the moment. Many practitioners say that walking meditation actually helps them achieve even greater awareness than conventional meditation, and that it's even easier to reach a state of mindfulness and awareness while walking, as opposed to sitting still.

Scientific discoveries supporting the benefits of meditation are spurring this mindfulness movement. The advantages of walking these winding paths are gaining attention in other disciplines beside health and well-being, and spirituality. Recently, business programs are using labyrinths to encourage a gentler, approachable, and authentic manner in leadership training. Educational institutions are adopting labyrinths to promote mindfulness and quiet reflection in teaching and learning.

. . .

In an attempt to find the average number of thoughts a person has in one day, I googled "number of thoughts per day." One result indicated our brains produce twelve thousand to fifty thousand thoughts per day, depending on how "deep" a thinker the person is. Philosopher Dr. Deepak Chopra suggested we have sixty thousand to eighty thousand thoughts daily.[22]

22   "The 70,000 Thoughts per Day Myth?," *Neuroskeptic* (blog), May 9, 2012, blogs.discovermagazine.com/neuroskeptic/2012/05/09/the-70000-thoughts-per-day-myth/.

Although this data is not measurable, the point is that we have too many thoughts a day. Living in a world addicted to thoughts, we have overactive brains that interfere with healthy functioning. We become fidgety, unable to rest fully, and struggle to achieve restorative sleep.

Browsing through a medical journal, I came across the term *monkey brain* in an article written by a psychiatrist. As soon as I read about this phenomenon—where overactive brains are difficult to calm as they are overflowing with thoughts—I knew immediately that she was describing my mind. Soon, I discovered I was not alone. There are many others who are like me.

The goal of mindfulness meditation is not to rid ourselves of all thoughts, as it is impossible to empty our minds. Mindfulness is not about stopping the mind, or stopping the thoughts, either. Mindfulness is about letting the thoughts be present, but not allowing them take charge.

To quiet and still the mind, we need to be gentle with ourselves. Some people are able to meditate by focusing on their breaths. It is simple for them to observe each breath, as it moves in and out of the body. They can effortlessly perceive the details of the each inhalation and exhalation, the air flowing in and out of the nose along with the each sensation in the body. However, others find this difficult. It is best to do what feels right for you.

The most effective way to meditate is to observe our thoughts and let them drift, like clouds high up into the sky. This awareness process allows us to learn and sort the thoughts occupying our minds. We want to keep the healthy and desirable thoughts—the ones that are positive, creative, insightful, healing, compassionate, connecting, and so forth. When we watch our thoughts, they lose their power, along with the emotions that are attached to them.

We need to set aside the time required to pay attention with care and discernment to what is occurring in our immediate experience. Being present means immersing ourselves in the here and now, and letting go of our constant preoccupations. It is about becoming more aware, alert, and awake to the fullness of the immediate moment. By completely immersing ourselves in the present moment, we receive the gift of a clear mind. We slow down our minds when we observe our thoughts without judgment, allow them to pass by, and do not engage them. Over time, this practice widens the gap between each thought, leaving a sweet spot of total relaxation and interconnectedness with the universe.

Meditation is about nurturing that area, growing it so that we spend more time in it. You want to be in this sacred space as much as possible. This is the place where human potential lies. Healing, letting go, and forgiveness are possible, allowing us to move forward.

· · ·

There was one week where I participated in extra step and Zumba aerobic classes. This resulted in hard, tight gluteus maximus muscles, which are the large muscles—about the size of a tennis ball—in the buttocks. When I could no longer ignore the discomfort, I had to make time for stretching exercises to relax the muscles and alleviate the pain. The tightness would have otherwise distracted me like a persistent toothache. As if it's a tight, overused muscle, you can also quiet the overactive mind, with the gentle attention of silence and stillness of walking meditation.

· · ·

*Turn your face to the sun and the shadows fall behind you.*
— MAORI PROVERB

In an effort to be objective about the number of negative thoughts a person has in one day, I googled "number of negative thoughts per day." The results were that an estimated 70 to 80 percent of our daily thoughts are negative.[23] This may be an unreliable finding, but the idea is we have too many negative thoughts throughout the day.

Negativity thrives in our society. Those who are aware of the psychological values of optimism can consciously frame a situation through a lens of beauty and opportunity. Adverse thinking, like cobwebs in the mind, can take days to sweep clean.

A lack of calm awareness of our body, mind, and feelings on a daily basis breeds a chaotic, directionless life. Undesirable emotions like fear, pain, worry, and anger spin dark clouds in our heads, dampen our spirits, and unconsciously drain us of energy, impacting health and well-being. In stillness, in silence, in observing our thoughts, negativity diminishes and has less impact.

We are told this process should be easy, but it is challenging to achieve for most people. The habitual practice of walking labyrinths helps us to remain productive amid conflicts, differences, and stress in our modern world. When achieved, the condition of the mind becomes clearer and effective. It is as if our physical body becomes light and free surrounded by brightness, our mind content and peaceful in the present moment. We become conscious of our bodies, actions, speech, and mind, whether we are eating, walking, or speaking.

23  George Dvorsky, "Managing Your 50,000 Daily Thoughts," *Sentient Developments* (blog), March 19, 2007, www.sentientdevelopments. com/2007/03/managing-your-50000-daily-thoughts.html

# Be Present

*Your true home is in the here and the now.*
— Thich Nhat Hanh

Our modern culture today suggests that outward activity is what matters. Paradoxically, there is also a massive quest for healthy self-understanding, deepening spiritual consciousness, and community-grounding spirituality outside of institutions such as churches. An enormous number of people are asking questions and seeking meaningful ways of existence. Yoga, Reiki, and non-denominational spiritual groups are attracting diverse people seeking an enlightened path. Walking labyrinths is about getting in touch with oneself, learning to go inward, discovering oneself, reflecting on what is important, being in the moment, and experiencing what that is all about.

New labyrinth-walkers look at the pattern on the floor and are afraid of becoming lost, of not finding their way out, despite instructions saying labyrinths are vastly unlike mazes. They seem to initially relate to a labyrinth as a maze, until a facilitator or someone with knowledge of labyrinths guides them through the process of letting go and trusting the process. Typically, after completing one walk and noticing its impact, the beginner walker wants to do more walks.

In a workshop for staff at a local college, I observed a middle-aged, petite secretary wearing a long-sleeved red sweater and polyester black pants who walked briskly, scurrying along its paths like a small animal anxious to return home with its finds. She told me that she is a very impatient person, usually rushing through life. She shared she has learned the need to slow down and be in the moment from walking the labyrinth.

Although it is difficult for us to grasp this, moments are all we have. We can't change yesterday or control tomorrow. Being present is a healthy way to live. Meditation is about coming back into the senses, into our selves. Learning to be in the moment, in the present, is a skill. Moments are fleeting. Moments ripe. Taste them. Be aware of them.

## Tame the Chattering Mind

*Little by little, through patience and repeated*
*effort, the mind will become stilled in the Self.*
— HINDU SCRIPTURE

Our minds race with things we must do, with memories that linger, with worries about the future that we have no control over. These endless thoughts about everything and nothing, yesterday and tomorrow, bury deep the present moment, making it untouchable. Like the heavy and thick fog covering the landscape outside, we are unable to clearly hear our own small voice or see the spaces in between our interactions.

Walking meditation helps us to connect with the present, hear our small voices, and feel the stillness our bodies crave. In the profound relaxation and serenity, we gain perspective and insight into our situation.

Thich Nhat Hanh, a Buddhist monk, writes about helping a boat full of Vietnamese refugees escape political persecution.[24] When the ship arrived in the Port of Singapore, they were given

24 Thich Nhat Hanh, *The Long Road Turns to Joy: A Guide to Walking Meditation* (Delhi, India: Full Circle, 1996).

twenty-four hours to leave. Not knowing what to do and unable to sleep from anxiety bordering on panic, Thich Nhat Hanh performed walking meditation all night. By morning, in the space of peace and relaxation, an answer came to him. Meditation was the way for him to see the light in a sea of darkness. It is when we are tranquil that we can be crystal clear in our exploration for the right solutions.

## Crystallize Alertness

On January 23, 2014, like other days, I was as tired as fading sunlight. Having transcribed several mental images, the long day's work had lost its color and vibrancy. My mind was groggy, like morning fog, and my body sluggish, apathetic, and unproductive. I drank a hot cup of tea with honey, mindful of each flavorful sip, but the dull, gray sleepiness would not vanish. Wanting to continue writing, I decided to walk the labyrinth to re-energize.

Down the stairs on our patio, a six-circuit concentric labyrinth of yellow and gray pavers awaited me. The cool, fresh air, massaging my face like tiny fingers, tingled lusciously. Deep breaths filled every lobe of my lungs. My body lightened as I walked the circular path beneath the hazy orange horizon. Alertness returned, while small birds chirped in the background. The walk along the winding path in the chilly air washed away my body and mental fatigue, like ocean waves carrying away debris from the shoreline. Awakening the senses, I was able to continue writing with delicious enthusiasm for a few more hours.

Walking the labyrinth is invigorating and helpful in building concentration. When we are tired or sluggish, walking can be invigorating. The act of moving our legs in strides not only revitalizes our body, but also our mood and attitude. The sensations of walking in the labyrinth are a robust and powerful moving meditation.

## Discover Insights

I was at a trade show when a middle-aged gentleman with silver-rimmed glasses asked questions about the warm, wooden finger labyrinths I had on display. Our conversation was initially about the logistics: What is the diameter of the labyrinths? How are they used? What type of labyrinths are these? How much are they? As the passerby became comfortable with me, he wanted to know more about the labyrinth in Fleetwood Park. The bearded man with bone-white hair, messy as haystacks, then shared his experience about a workshop he attended in San Francisco.

This man finally shared a discovery. He said in a soft voice, "You can't demand a mystical experience." With his shoes off in socked feet and an inward focus, he was ready for a "mystical" experience. Just as he was about to enter this patterned sacred space, a roaring sound competed for his senses. He soon discovered a gardener with a leaf blower strapped to his back cleaning the surroundings. It was at that moment that he realized that you can't demand a mystical experience. This is how the labyrinth offers lessons each time we walk it.

# Mirror the Soul

*The unexamined life is not worth living.*
— Socrates

We become aware of our thoughts, emotions, and memories while walking the labyrinth. Insights can be gained by paying attention to them. I remember the observations I have of a participant in one of my workshops.

The college instructor with frizzy hair and bare feet negotiated the labyrinth with trepidation. She had recently recovered from bunion surgery. With a limp and sad voice, she said she needed to figure out what to do with her unhappy life. However, she told me later she found glimpses of joy in the labyrinth, which would encourage her to continue her pursuit of purpose in her life.

In the same workshop, another participant shared her story. She claimed, with a broad smile, she did not know what it meant to be in the moment. The thirty-something, dressed in a white T-shirt and blue jeans, added she was unable to separate her inner sphere from the external world. Time spent in the labyrinth enabled her to reflect and turn inward, assisting her to experience what it means to be.

The labyrinth prompts us to remain open and to receive possibilities. I invite you to join me for a labyrinth experience.

Please use a lap labyrinth or the labyrinth on page 51 of this book if a floor or ground labyrinth is not available. Join me in tracing the path of the lap or paper labyrinth with your finger.

# Find Deep Peace

*There are times when we stop. We sit still. We listen*
*and breezes from a whole other world begin to whisper.*
— JAMES CARROLL

As you gradually become adept at observing your thoughts, pay particular attention to the gaps between each thought. This space is where the universe resides. It is edgeless, boundless, and infinite, filled with love, peace, and connection. It is in this space that a deep sense of interconnectedness, tranquillity, and belonging is experienced.

It was pitch black when we looked out the window. The day's busy-ness was nearly over, dinner cooked and eaten, dishes washed and put away, all of us satisfied that the repetitive tasks of the day were done—the arrival of night welcomed. I was ready to put my legs up and drink a cup of tea in silence, when my husband, David, said, "Let's go for a walk," holding a faded blue sleeping bag under his arms. Hesitantly, our two preteen children and I followed suit.

The skies were dark black, with nary a trace of light. The width of the yellow light shining from his handheld flashlight lit the way. We walked what seemed like a thousand miles. At times we held our breath, winding down a declining, uneven path, then up a larger hill with enormous cracks in the road. Each step was increasingly enhanced by the roar of the nearby ocean announcing its invitation, by way of the delicate, salty air mixed with the summer night's chill.

As the crashes of the ocean waves grew loud, we approached a cliff overlooking the ocean. My husband gingerly unfolded the sleeping bag and motioned for us to lie down. The four of us lay flat on our backs against the hard, cool earth. Looking up, the sky was no longer shrouded in thick blackness; instead, it was filled with millions of tiny twinkling stars commingling with a full, luminous moon. There we lay, in an awe-filled silence, fully taking in the universe's essence. Its enormity filled our spirits, like oil for a burning lamp. The stillness grew in our bodies, echoing the small voice we were meeting once again. Deep peace. Connection. Love.

Meditation alters our state of consciousness—like this story of taking in fully what the moment and nature had to offer. This deep awareness of our inner sensations connects us to our deepest essence. Once we master mindfulness, this higher order of consciousness is accessible. Our hyperactive brain discovers peace and bliss when we frequently attain this state.

Chapter 6

# Transformational Stories of Growth and Change

*The wound is the place where the Light enters you.*
— RUMI

## Heal Grief

WE MOURN WHEN THERE IS LOSS. A FEW EXAMPLES OF LOSS include opportunity, employment, identity, or health and well-being. However, with the passing away of someone you love profoundly, grief lasts forever. Over time, we learn to manage sorrow, live with it like a change in seasons, learn to move forward. The sadness first appears every day, constantly preoccupying the mind, body, and spirit. As time passes, it appears less. It becomes less overwhelming and unmanageable.

The aching sadness and anger that formed the solid mass in my mid-abdomen did not subside. Like a petulant child, *grief* screamed for attention. Pushing her further away hindered my thoughts and focus, drained my energy, interfered with my ability to be productive.

*Grief* had arrived two days earlier, lingering and nudging for

66

conversation. A sudden onslaught of work and fatigue made her an unwanted visitor. However, she remained, played hide-and-seek, disappeared, and reappeared periodically throughout the day. Drawing air into the depths of my lungs briefly quieted and tamed *grief*; however, it did not heal the reawakening of the acute injury that resulted from the severance of a profound love relationship.

It began one morning when I woke up to see my mother in the mirror. I saw her eyes, nose, and mouth looking back at me. Like a tsunami, anguish and affection flooded my body and soul, as her big warm smile with small, perfect, straight white teeth looked at me. I wondered why she died. The physicians who attended to her offered an overwhelming detailed technical explanation; however, the reasons were not satisfying. Could they have done more? Did they give up too soon? Had they tried everything in their power, experience, and knowledge?

The thought of them seeing her as an insignificant immigrant woman with little value hastening their giving up increased my mistrust. They discouraged an autopsy and I never questioned them, as I felt my mother had suffered enough. Further, I wanted to minimize their insensitive and callous touching of her body. I wanted my mother to have peace. It had been a lengthy process of doctors' visits, lab tests, and medication prescriptions, leading to her sudden death. I knew she was weary.

That was more than twenty-four years ago. I have never forgotten her. I see her everywhere. My mother's image appears in all she loved—blood-red roses in Stanley Park; full peony blossoms in our garden; ripe yellow-orange papayas and apricots in the summer; and blackish-red plums on hot days. Her love shines in the more than one hundred dresses she sewed for my children, each dress uniquely adorned with an assortment of colorful buttons, ribbons, and appliqués of balloons and flowers.

*Grief* visited me on the coldest day in January. Under dull skies with a freezing wind, I slowly entered the labyrinth seeking solace. I walked shouldering the weight of sad emptiness. Left, right, left, right—left, heel to ball of foot; right, heel to ball of foot—repeating slowly. The cold air felt crunchy in my nostrils, like the frozen frost on the ground. In the center of this sacred path, I felt gratitude.

My mother's legacy is about enduring love. I am thankful that she fed me, dressed me, and loved me as if I could do no wrong. The wisdom in my body cannot be found in books; this intelligence came from my mother, the petite, thin woman with the largest smile. I followed in her footsteps; I too fed my children, dressed and loved them, as if they could do no wrong. Others have told me what I already know, that my daughters will feed their children, dress and love them, as if they could do no wrong.

. . .

*She was no longer wrestling with the grief, but could sit down with it as a lasting companion and make it a sharer in her thoughts.*
— GEORGE ELIOT

I received this story from a fellow labyrinth journeyer, who discovered a new understanding while walking the labyrinth. Richard's transition into retirement began when his brother suddenly died of a heart attack. After decades of nursing the sick and spreading prophetic words about wellness, Richard was looking forward to the exploration and self-discoveries in this new phase of life. His brother's death meant an abrupt detour from his anticipated plans.

Now, there was a funeral to organize, out-of-town family members to host, an apartment that must be emptied and cleaned, and the last will and testament administered. Once again the well-remembered busy-ness, like running on the treadmill, kept him focused on his "must do" list for days.

The day following the funeral, he walked a newly painted labyrinth on parachute fabric. His sister and sister-in-law accompanied him. Exhausted and in turmoil, he led his visitors along the labyrinth's winding path in silence. The women were willing to follow Richard's footsteps. Without explanations or questions, the three wound its path together.

Shortly after entering the uni-cursal path, Richard began to cry. His loud, heavy sobs were difficult to witness. He took deep breaths to muffle the cries. Tears poured from his swollen eyes down his reddened face and squashed mouth. His torso shook to the rhythm of his sobs. He continued to walk with his face buried inside his elbow.

By the time he reached the center, all of a sudden—he felt the heaviness lift from his shoulders. A wave of relief caressed his entire body. Pulses of joy danced lightly on his skin. Air flowed effortlessly into his lungs. He stayed in the center long enough to realize that he had—at that moment—transcended his grief.

Richard continued to walk slowly with inward attention, one foot steadily in front of the other. As he exited the labyrinth, he knew he had said good-bye to his brother. He missed him and did not like that his brother had died; however, he accepted that his brother's death, like the nature of all life, is fragile, and that death is inevitable. In a fleeting thought of *memento mori*, he pondered his own mortality.

# Transcend Despair

*Try to love the questions themselves. . . . Live the questions now. Perhaps, then, someday far in the future, you will gradually, without even noticing, live your way into the answer.*
— RAINER MARIA RILKE

Despair is like sinking into the dark, bottomless hole, barely hanging onto the thread of life, going nowhere; the gateway to life is closing. You are in this space of not knowing where up is, where down is, directionless, going nowhere, not knowing which route to take, when being is overwhelming.

Stay here. Don't run away, or cover, or mask your feelings. Stay here just long enough to move on. Moving on is the single healthy solution to being alive. Stay here to see clearly, to decide which path to take. Perspective will soon present itself.

Walk the labyrinth, keep walking, and trust that a decision, a direction will appear. Peace will arrive soon enough. Answers will come when you ask for them, when you pay attention to your body and inner voice. Take a walk; use the opportunity to ground yourself. Breathing in, feel your feet touch the earth, breathing out, feel the peace and spaciousness mixed with despair. Notice your feet, lifting the left one, then the right one. Feel the pain; it is the path to healing and wholeness.

I met Rebecca at a conference, who told me a story about Andrew, a young man who was a guest at her bed and breakfast. Rebecca had created a large Chartres labyrinth with yellowish-green boxwood hedges on her enormous property. Andrew was intrigued by its winding paths. He asked Rebecca about the labyrinth. To prepare him for the walk, she walked the lunations on the outside of the circle. Holding the space for him, she walked the outer perimeter of the labyrinth, while Andrew made his way on the winding path. Rebecca provided a neutral territory for him to just be. She continued on the outside of the circle without judgment, criticism, or blame. She provided a stable, solid ground for him to be completely where he was at that moment. When Andrew was close to finishing the walk, Rebecca moved away and waited for him in the garden.

Later, Rebecca asked if there was anything she could help him with, whether he wished to talk about his experience. Andrew said that it had been an extremely enlightening and lightening experience. A load he had carried for decades had been lifted. He shared that his sister had committed suicide, and he had walked hoping for some understanding and peace.

His sister spoke to him in the labyrinth, telling him he did not need to carry the guilt or weight—that she was fine and he should get on with his life. Andrew was amazed by the experience. As the message sunk in, he became happier and relieved. He was grateful for the facilitated labyrinth walk.


## Abate Anxiety

*Go within every day and find the inner strength*
*so that the world will not blow your candle out.*
— KATHERINE DUNHAM

I knew that Todd, the slender, brown-haired man, was mad at me, although I did not know his reasons. Across the room, he barely looked at me, refused to acknowledge me, his presence like a big colorless elephant in the room. I was uncomfortable but had to self-manage despite the increasing anxiety. The evening continued as others in the room listened, laughed, and clapped to the singer's melancholy songs and stories. Time passed as the South Asian performer strummed his guitar in the dimly lit room. It took effort to ignore the uneasiness, as Todd and I are acquaintances in several social circles.

The silent elephant dissipated into the room as the musician sang into the night. I could almost feel the warmth from the battery-operated candles. Over hot green tea and gluten-free cranberry muffins, I met and socialized with others who were seeking a temporary community for the evening.

I would have found this situation difficult years earlier. Now, I was able to disconnect from it and observe myself, a detachment, which I attribute to the practice of mindfulness and meditation. I am much better at simultaneously distinguishing my internal and external world, and responding consciously, rather than reacting without thought. Awareness is the first step in remaining calm in situations that are difficult to make sense of. As Viktor Frankl describes it, "Between stimulus and response, there is a *space*. In that space is our power to choose our response. In our response lies our growth and our freedom."

I never did find out why Todd was annoyed with me; I did offer twice to meet with him for conversation at a cafe. He declined both invitations. Although I am curious about his behavior and our awkward interaction lacks closure, I chose not to put further energy into this circumstance and to move on.

• • •

About 2006, I was traveling in China, and I had to travel alone by bus from the city of Zhongshan to the city of Zhuhai, a twenty-minute car ride away. Since I was unsure that my elementary

Cantonese would be helpful in asking for directions if I became lost, my friend thought it a good idea to write the name and address of the hotel on a piece of paper to show the bus driver. As soon as I boarded the bus, I asked the slightly built bus driver, in broken Chinese, to stop at the bus stop nearest to the location written on the piece of white paper.

Without looking at or acknowledging me, and expressing surprising irritation, he gestured his arm for me to sit down, as if he was waving away a bee. I sat on a nearby empty seat and observed the roads, traffic, and passersby. Ten minutes passed when I decided that I had best approach the bus driver again. I wobbled on the moving bus up to him and pulled the scrap of paper from my pocket. The driver again gazed straight ahead, groaned and motioned for me to go back to my seat. It was clear his intention was to ignore me.

Once again, I sat down. Another five minutes passed; I realized I was panicking as all the buildings suddenly became similar in size, color, and shape. Again, I approached the man, and again, he reacted with the same callous behavior. This time I said in English, "Please Mr. Bus Driver, be kind. When you are kind, good things will come to you." To my surprise, he said in resigned Mandarin Chinese, "Sit down, I will call you when we are there."

In two or three minutes, he looked into the bus's front mirror and called for me to get off. I was relieved and grateful that I was not lost. Years ago, I would have been nervous and worried in such a situation. Awareness and ability to remain calm—acquired through meditation—contributes to my capacity to manage situations that are difficult to make sense of.

# Awaken the Spirit

*Walking the labyrinth clears the mind and gives insights into
the spiritual journey. It urges action. It calms people in the throes
of life transitions. It helps them see their lives in the context of
a path, a pilgrimage. They realize that they are not human
beings on a spiritual path but spiritual beings on a human path.*
— Lauren Artress

Breanne, a kind, gentle woman, is a colleague who told me there
was a time in her life when she wanted to die. Living was too
miserable and painful. She was depressed for months at a time.
Married to an alcoholic, she was in a relationship that was a constant struggle. Loud fights and meaningless conversations emptied
her soul. Seldom was there peace or love in the home. One day,
she felt tired of living. She no longer saw any joy or purpose in
existing. She went down to the railway tracks with the intent of
jumping in front of a train to end it all. When she arrived there,
she realized she was terribly afraid; she was so full of fears. She
was even frightened of her shadow on the ground.

That episode was Breanne's first turning point in her life, which
led her to joining Al-Anon. It was at those meetings that she
learned a language to describe what was happening inside of her.
Words led to making meaning of the difficult relationship with her
husband and how his drinking behavior influenced her. She met
people who shared similar experiences as her. Conversations in
that supportive environment opened up a whole new world to her.

With regular attendance at the group meetings, she found the
courage to not to react, to instead understand her husband and
to see the good in him as the first steps to managing their relationship and healing herself. Over the years, she became involved
in various spiritual groups. Each one offered her more words to

weave into her personal theology. While the situation at home changed little, she had transformed phenomenally. Three years into her spiritual awakening, Breanne became conscious of herself as a spiritual being. "I was more aware, more joyful, more patient, and more compassionate. There was even laughter in my life," Breanne confided.

Since her husband died, she has remarried. Today, she talks about the magic of believing and forgiveness that is so necessary in every healthy relationship. She continues to say that love follows when there is awareness, acceptance, assertiveness, responsibility for our own behaviors, and respect for our own feelings.

The labyrinth is deeply special to her. Her habitual work with labyrinths deepened and expanded her spirituality. "The labyrinth has helped me to experience and deepen those good inward states more intensely and for a longer period of time," Breanne affirmed. She now works as a spiritual practitioner, who specializes in personal development. The labyrinth is a process like life. It is full of turning points.

## Make Major Life Transitions

*And the day came when the risk to remain tight in the bud was more painful than the risk it took to blossom.*
— ANAÏS NIN

Today, thirteen years after I was first introduced to labyrinths, I think about how fortunate that I am to have received so many spiritual offerings from working with labyrinths. The labyrinth was introduced to me, and I have introduced it to over one thousand people.

All of us, in one way or another, who explore the values of

labyrinths are seekers of truth, peace, and purposeful living. This diverse group of people—even amidst differences and conflict—can be gracious. They give and receive with their energies to create peaceful and warm relationships.

When we are deeply aware of how our spirits are expressed in the way we live and work, we are consciously creating effective and healthy relations.

Josie, a gentle and high-functioning person, is one of these people I have met through this community. At age forty, with a doctorate degree and an impressive list of publications in esteemed journals and magazines, she had reached assistant deanship at a prominent university. Her next step on the triangular organizational chart is dean, a prestigious position. She owns a mortgage-free house and has a caring extended family, which she regularly connects with. However, unhappy and unwell in the aggressively competitive, extremely individualistic, and highly work-driven environment, her energy and spirit were dampened; she was unable to find enjoyment or see anything positive in her life. This sad existence veiled every aspect of her daily life. The wake-up call came when her lower back pain became excruciating. She was no longer able to sit or work. Frequent visits to the physician and many other health-care professionals led to poor results and discussions of back surgery.

Falling apart with a way of being that had spun out of control led Josie to a path for purpose, healing, and direction. She now does walking meditation on the labyrinth regularly. Its winding path sustained her as she meandered through the changes externally imposed on her as well as the ones she created herself. Meditation has helped her find tranquillity during these transitions and transformations. Today, after years of personal development, she enjoys physical health, experiences inner peace, and newfound awareness that help her explore new directions in life.

# Become Whole

*We must be willing to let go of the life we*
*planned so as to have the life that is waiting for us.*
— JOSEPH CAMPBELL

My colleague Sophia, a confident and achievement-oriented woman, also loves labyrinths. We both work professionally in the discipline of organizational development. She shared her story with me when she found out that I was writing a book.

The November sun shone bold and bright high up in the white-blue sky. Its valiant attempt could not warm the temperature of late fall. The cold ocean breeze lingered, clinging to everything it touched. Gloved hands and heads covered with woolen hats could not escape its sharp bite. Subtle flavors of rotting leaves and salt air intermingled with the clean, fresh scent. Semi-bare trees dressed with brown, yellow, and red leaves stood like brushstrokes on canvases of picturesque landscapes.

The large labyrinth constructed of crudely mowed lawn and mud-packed rocks stood unassuming in an open field. Overlooking the sea with its back to the forest, the labyrinth invited curious onlookers. What was this round pathway? What did it do? What was it for? How do I walk it? What happens when I walk it?

Sophia was introduced to the labyrinth, one and a half years after her initial diagnosis of cancer. The numerous visits to physicians, specialists, and other health-care professionals drained her physically and challenged her spirits. "I had just come out of the cancer stuff, including the chemotherapy and radiation. My hair grew back and I had lost so much weight," she recalled in a clear, firm voice.

The malignancy tried to become her; it had invaded her cells and taken her identity. As a director for a prominent city hospital, she was a key player in the organization, responsible for leading major projects and making influential decisions that impacted hundreds of people. The tumor shattered her whole being and was winning in turning her into its prey. She was wearily aware of its need for attention twenty-four hours a day.

The fight to not become a person with cancer was a muted one. Well-meaning friends, family members, and colleagues spoke of the cancer whenever they met. Sophia said, "I didn't want to carry the cancer-survivor identity. I was resistant to the whole survivor-ship identity."

On that brisk, sunny November afternoon, Sophia was invited to walk the labyrinth with a group of eight other college instructors at a conference. It was her first experience. They each followed one another around the outside of the labyrinth to "warm" it. As soon as Sophia entered the labyrinth, "I was meditating right away. I was letting go of stuff as I was walking toward the center." Sophia followed the others' footsteps, with each step along a path that looped left and right, leading to the center. She described the life-giving nature of walking labyrinths. "Things became magical when I was in the center. A flame burned on the inside of me rather than being on the outside of me. The flame meant the Supreme Being or God was with me, or whatever you want to call it. Sometimes the spirit was leading me, sometimes it was not there. Sometimes it was ahead of me. Sometimes it was in me."

Sophia's thoughts became hopeful and optimistic as she remained in the center. Her body moved with lightness and ease. She said, "One of the things I liked about walking the labyrinth is that I became energized by the whole sense of life that comes of it. It is a life-giving and enlightening experience."

Sophia comes out a transformed person each time she walks the labyrinth. She eloquently summarizes the benefits of walking labyrinths: "I would like it in my life to help me to manage anxiety and stay healthy. I hunt all over the place to walk labyrinths."

## Create a New Story

*Out beyond ideas of wrongdoing and rightdoing,
there is a field. I'll meet you there.*
— RUMI

Amidst the hubbub of stereo music, Vanessa shared how she uses labyrinths in her life. The tunes intermixed with the voices of people to provide privacy as intimate stories were told. The fragrance of fresh coffee jostled distant memories. The cozy and warm cafe invited the sharing of stories between old friends.

Slowly sipping the hot herbal tea, Vanessa described how walking the labyrinth is a valuable process in her life's work. Her face lit up and she sat up straight when she told me about the labyrinth and how she used it to make life-changing decisions. She described the circuitous path as an amazing and powerful catalyst to change.

Vanessa knew she could not stay in her decaying, isolating marriage of fifteen years. The questions that raced through her head intensified her fear of leaving, yet she no longer wanted to be married to Tyler. She didn't know when to leave. How to leave? Where would she go? What about the children? What would she do?

It was a Saturday afternoon, a time she typically visited St. Paul's Anglican Church. Built of red bricks, the familiar building was a short drive from her home. There was comfort in her body as soon as she entered the gym, where a Chartres labyrinth is painted on the hardwood floor. The lights were dim, and through the narrow stained-glass windows, the overcast sky encouraged inward attention.

Vanessa paused to watch the few walkers on the path. She mindfully took three deep breaths, gradually breathing in and slowly exhaling. As she took her first steps into the labyrinth, she waited for her inner voice to speak, to offer her instructions. "Okay, I am open to any answers you may have. I need to know where I am going. I need to know what to do." She surrendered to the act of walking to find her solutions.

When she reached the center, the answers came to her. Eight months later, she lives in a new city, has embarked on a new job, and sorted the children's living arrangements. The labyrinth has become a meaningful and significant tool for her during these chaotic times of change.

It took eight years to leave Tyler and find new love for her life. Now, Vanessa is established, well into living on her own, and is not interested in a new relationship. There is a new kind of routine and rhythm to her life. She has created a day-to-day work-life structure that makes her happy. She likes her newfound confidence and sense of direction with freedom.

Gone are the habitual confusion, tension, and silent arguments with Tyler. She likes the life she has created.

Meeting Adam was a reluctant, accidental encounter. She met him while cycling down a hill to complete an errand. Adam was standing there, as if he was waiting for her. When she came around a corner of the street, he greeted her in a surprisingly friendly and approachable manner. That was the beginning of their relationship.

Four years slipped before Vanessa introduced Adam to the labyrinth at Fenn's Lodge. She entered first, followed by Adam. When they both arrived in the center, Adam said to her, "We are going to get married here."

Six months later, beneath blue skies, the couple, dressed in their best, brought their families and friends along with a justice of the peace to the labyrinth. This gathering was about celebrating and sanctifying their partnership.

Their loved ones circled the labyrinth, while Vanessa entered the labyrinth followed by Adam. The marriage official was waiting for them in the center. When the couple arrived in the center, they faced each other and placed their left hand to their hearts, while their right hands touched. After the blessings from the marriage commissioner, they took turns declaring the vows they wrote for each other. A sand dollar was broken to release the dovelike particles inside.

The couple left the center and the witnesses, one by one, entered the twisting path touching hands. It was like a joyous dance rhythmically played out on an enormous, outdoor circle. Seemingly, to complete the ceremony, a pair of eagles happened to circle high up in the skies above them.

Today, both Adam and Vanessa continue to purposely seek and walk labyrinths. Walking labyrinths has become an important part of their life. Pursuing a meaningful life requires constant creativity, because the paths will not always be obvious or easy to follow.

Chapter 7

# Science Befriends
# Ancient Practice

*Absence of evidence is not evidence of absence.*
— CARL SAGAN

TWENTY-FOUR YEARS AGO, THE YEAR MY MOTHER DIED, I was deeply distraught. As I write this, images of my mother, the circumstances, our relationship along with the emotions of loss, however distant in time, continue to play out in my body and mind. I remember finding solace, cradled by a hammock made of colorful cotton netting, staring at our yellowish-green bamboo hedge swaying from side to side. The thick bamboo stalks, moving in unison, synchronized with the warm breeze like a troupe of dancers under the clear blue sky, soothed my soul. At the time, intense grief, nature, and back-and-forth eye movements following the bamboo provided healing in ways that I did not understand and for which I had no explanation.

Years later, I stumbled on an article in a medical journal at work about eye movement desensitization and reprocessing (EMDR), a fairly new, nontraditional type of psychotherapy. EMDR uses a person's own rapid, rhythmic eye movements to dampen the power of emotionally charged memories of past traumatic events.[25] On that day, I discovered a name for the feelings and sensations I felt on that summer day, with memories of my mother, beside the trees, under the heavens.

*   *   *

How does the labyrinth work exactly in creating the shifts that people describe? Research studies indicate the common effects from walking labyrinths, as linked to on the Labyrinth Society website (labyrinthsociety.org/).[26] These common benefits are themed under two categories: physical and "state of mind." They include these descriptors:

- Feel less agitation, stress, and anxiety; replenish energy; reclaim calm

- Be more clear, open, peaceful, relaxed, focused, centered, quiet, reflective

- Nurture the soul; decrease somatic stress and worry; have steady blood pressure; have higher physical and mental relaxation; improve overall wellness and health

- Facilitate a calming meditative state that heightens intuition, creativity, and a shift in consciousness

---

25  "EMDR: Eye Movement Desensitization and Reprocessing," *WebMD*, www.webmd.com/mental-health/emdr-what-is-it.

26  John W. Rhodes, "Commonly Reported Effects of Labyrinth Walking," *Labyrinth Pathways*, July 2008, zdi1.zd-cms.com/cms/res/files/382/Commonly-Reported-Effects-of-Labyrinth Walking-Labyrinth-Pathways-July-2008-3.pdf.

. . .

Regardless of the fact that scientific progress has tremendously improved our current health and longevity, science does not have explanations for everything. Although the mainstream scientific community has not yet recognized, accepted, and embraced the benefits of labyrinths, like my accidental discovery about EMDR, the experience had validity long before a scientific label was available. Our experiences and responses in our body, mind, and spirit have legitimacy. Responsibility for our well-being mandates that we seek to discover the modalities that can help us to heal, to be whole. As such, we should put effort into our healing—to listen, incorporate, trust, and be open to knowledge from ourselves that shows us healing processes, however unique the experiences may be.

Physical and spiritual health is integrated. "Just as a candle cannot burn without fire, men cannot live without a spiritual life," Buddha said. Man has artificially created the division separating these two domains. I believe we have given far too much authority and power to health care and religious professionals. The relationship between the impact of health and spirituality has not received the attention they deserve in higher education.

I believe walking meditation in labyrinths is a powerful yet simple process, which, with consistent practice, can improve many areas of life, including health and well-being, business, and relationships, and possibly even facilitate world peace.

. . .

Robert Sapolsky, a neurobiologist and researcher at Stanford University, discovered that stress actually shrinks our brains, adds fat to our bellies, and unravels our DNA strands. Our chromosomes are made up of deoxyribonucleic acid (DNA), which encodes the genetic instructions used in the development and functioning of all known living organisms. In a television documentary called *Stress: Portrait of a Killer*, Sapolsky described the impact of stress on the human body.[27] Our human body, like those of other animals, is designed to fight, take flight, or be eaten by predators in the jungle. The chemicals released in our brains channel all our energies into doing these things in split seconds.

Although most of us no longer live in the wild where we fear being hunted or need to kill for food, these defense mechanisms persist in our concrete world. Difficulties in tolerating situations like workplace conflicts, traffic jams, or domestic problems produce the same chemicals in our brains, creating the same "fight or flight" effect on our bodies as it did long ago when we were hunters and gatherers. Over time, these chemicals produce an overtaxed stress response that deteriorates our physiology, becoming a major contributor to illness. Imagine what can happen with a smaller brain as our vital organ, and fractured DNA as the blueprint to our biological makeup. These are essential components that keep us alive!

The human species, despite our intelligence for solving countless problems, has turned these basic survival mechanisms—the stress response—against itself. We struggle with life's leftovers and worry about a tomorrow that has not yet arrived. Instead, we need to live more in the moment, to be mindful. Walking labyrinths still our thoughts—neither grasping at them nor pushing them away. Walking meditation facilitates taking in fully the present moment.

27    See the website of the television documentary at killerstress.stanford.edu.

Numerous studies support the benefits of meditation and other meditative practices such as yoga, prayer, tai chi, and the like. At one time, it was believed that our brain had developed fully by our twenties. However, new scientific findings about meditation and brain changes show that our brains continue to develop through the experiences we have. Neuroscientists have made discoveries identifying the positive effects meditation has on both the structure and function of the brains.[28] Studies have found that meditation produces:

- Better attention, cognitive flexibility, and memory

- Greater self-awareness and self-regulation

- Reduced anxiety, and improved mental well-being and empathy for others

- Increased social support and a sense of purpose in life, and decreased illness and depression[29]

. . .

Stress has become ubiquitous, impacting our health and well-being, playing a significant role in cancer, heart conditions, chronic pain, infertility, and autoimmune diseases. It is estimated that 60 to 90 percent of doctor visits are for stress-related

28   P. Vestergaard-Poulsen, M. van Beek, J. Skewes, C. R. Bjarkam, M. Stubberup, J. Bertelsen, and A. Roepstorff, "Long-Term Meditation Is Associated with Increased Gray Matter Density in the Brain Stem," *Neuroreport.* 2009;20(2):170–74.

29   B. L. Fredrickson, M. A. Cohn, K. A. Coffey, J. Pek, and S. M. Finkel, "Open Hearts Build Lives: Positive Emotions, Induced through Loving-Kindness Meditation, Build Consequential Personal Resources," *Journal of Personality and Social Psychology*, 95(5):1045–62.

complaints.[30] Reducing stress prevents sickness and decreases the severity and level of illness. Dr. Benson-Henry's research studies find that focused walking-meditation and sitting-meditation are highly effective in eliciting the relaxation response that can result in a reduction in stress levels. The practice of meditation impacts health extensively by slowing heart and breath rates, decreasing blood pressure, loosening tight muscles, enabling improved sleep, and lessening episodes of chronic pain. Walking meditation in the labyrinth is a tool to reduce stress and increase personal resiliency when life presents us with physical and emotional challenges.

\* \* \*

Dr. Jon Kabat-Zinn, a medical researcher and educator, was able to replicate the positive results derived from mindfulness meditation. He learned about this meditation on a retreat led by Zen monk Thich Nhat Hanh. Hanh is a well-known leader and practitioner of walking meditation and a peace activist. Kabat-Zinn recognized the value of mindfulness in the treatment of chronic medical conditions and adapted the monk's teachings into a structured stress reduction program.[31]

For decades, the scientist and his colleagues have been conducting studies into mindfulness meditation on participants with medical issues ranging from chronic pain conditions to anxiety

---

30  "Published Research by Date," Benson-Henry Institute for Mind Body Medicine, Massachusetts General Hospital, www.bensonhenryinstitute.org/our-research/published-research.

31  Joanna Cheek, "Tune In: Being Mindful of the Now Can Lead to Good Health," *Vancouver Sun*, March 4, 2014, www.vancouversun.com/health/Tune +Being+mindful+lead+good+health/9574403/story.html.

and panic.[32] Participants in the program learn to see clearly the patterns of the mind. They learn to recognize when their mood is declining, and to break the link between negative mood and the negative thinking it would normally trigger. Participants develop the capacity to allow distressing mood, thoughts, and sensations to come and go, without having to battle with them. They eventually find they can stay in the moment without ruminating about the past or worrying about the future.

The researchers were able to consistently demonstrate that the participants develop increased psychological resiliency from mindfulness meditation, resulting in a heightened sense of self, better relationships, and improved functioning under stress. They took better care of themselves and as a result enjoyed improved health and well-being.

Millions of people from all walks of life—including health-care professionals, Google employees, and world business and political leaders—have discovered how to use their innate resources and abilities to respond effectively to stress, pain, and illness.[33] Imagine how mindfulness and walking meditation in the labyrinth can benefit you.

32  "History of MBSR," Center for Mindfulness in Medicine, Health Care, and Society, University of Massachusetts Medical School, www.umassmed.edu/cfm/stress-reduction/history-of-mbsr/.

33  Anderson Cooper, "Mindfulness," transcript of an episode of 60 Minutes, December 14, 2014, www.cbsnews.com/news/mindfulness-anderson-cooper-60-minutes/.

Chapter 8

# Walking the Labyrinth: Meditation for World Peace

*Be the change you wish to see in the world.*
— Unknown

I HAVE BEEN FACILITATING WORLD LABYRINTH DAY'S WALK as One at 1" in our Surrey community since 2012. It was absolutely exciting to see the large number of participants at our 2014 labyrinth walk. The number of people who came out for this event attests to the rising popularity of labyrinths. It was even more amazing to learn in the report from the Labyrinth Society that an estimated five thousand people celebrated the sixth annual World Labyrinth Day in more than twenty-four countries. Over three hundred people from different countries around the world responded to The Society's online survey, including in Canada, Argentina, Australia, the Bahamas, Belgium, Brazil, the Cayman Islands, Colombia, Costa Rica, Czech Republic, England, France, Germany, Ireland, Italy, Lithuania, Mexico, the Netherlands, Poland, Portugal, Scotland, South Africa, Spain, and the United States. People from all over the world walked labyrinths in public parks, churches, a maximum-security women's prison, and retreat centers, as well as many private labyrinths.

The Labyrinth Society, an organization in the United States, created World Labyrinth Day (WLD), occuring on the first Saturday of May. Their mission (as stated on their website) is "to support all those who create, maintain, and use labyrinths, and to serve the global community by providing education, networking, and opportunities to experience transformation."[34] On this day, people are encouraged to join others around the globe to walk a labyrinth. The intention is to generate, across the time zones, a wave of peaceful energy for the good of all.

At the end of 2013, feeling quite relaxed after the Christmas frenzy as December was coming to a close, I reflected on my work for the year and contemplated on what I would like to accomplish in the coming year. On that cold, frosty evening, just as the orange sun was fading into the horizon, the idea of designating a day in our community to promote peace was born. I sent an email to the city's clerk, requesting information on how to apply for a proclamation by the mayor. To my surprise, I quickly received a response. Over the next few months, a draft proclamation was reviewed and revised several times before the city representatives and I selected the final one. This final version of the proclamation was submitted to our mayor for consideration at the city council meeting on April 28, 2014.

At approximately 10 p.m., our mayor announced the proclamation, after the lengthy land-development debate ended. There were no drumrolls, no applause, and no fireworks, but I did feel accomplished for initiating this proclamation and following it through to success. The idea of setting aside differences one hour

34    "World Labyrinth Day," The Labyrinth Society, labyrinthsociety.org/world-labyrinth-day.

of each year to walk the labyrinth for peace is a deeply meaningful and noble endeavor. Peace extends to recognizing and acknowledging the contributions of *all*. We as a society are enriched by the diversity of people, cultures, philosophies, and religions.

In doing research for this book, I discovered there are large organizations that believe meditation may be a way to achieve world peace. Although I have not contemplated on this, I recall Margaret Mead's message, "Never doubt that a small group of thoughtful, committed citizens can change the world; indeed, it's the only thing that ever does."

Imagine if meditation can help a person to be tranquil, interact with the world calmly, and gain a greater feeling of serenity and harmony with the universe. Imagine the possibilities when the larger collective meditates for world peace and the betterment of all humanity. Imagine when people meditate for world peace to better the lives of people all over the world, go beyond, and take action. This may be the loftiest idea ever to some and possibly to many people; however, do consider the potential that by being at peace with ourselves, we are also helping to bring peace to the world. As Edward Everett Hale would say, "I am only one, but still I am one. I cannot do everything, but still I can do something; and because I cannot do everything, I will not refuse to do something that I can do."

CITY OF
SURREY
the future lives here.

# PROCLAMATION

## Surrey World Labyrinth Day: Walk as One at 1

### May 3, 2014

**WHEREAS**   Surrey is a community that is enriched by the diversity of people, cultures, philosophies, and religions, where the contributions of *all* are acknowledged and appreciated; and

**WHEREAS**   Peace, respect, and pluralism are fundamental characteristics of Surrey; and

**WHEREAS**   Diana Ng is the Community Leader, who successfully led the project, building the *first* public labyrinth in Greater Vancouver's Lower Mainland in partnership with the City of Surrey, the South Fraser Unitarian Congregation, and Minerva Innovations Consultancy. The labyrinth is located in Fleetwood Park, and is a Seven Circuit Classical Labyrinth, consisting of a 42 ft. diameter pathway that promotes mindfulness; and

**WHEREAS**   World Labyrinth Day is designed to bring people from all over the world together to walk labyrinths as one, to create a wave of peaceful energy and for the good of all washing across the time zones;

**NOW, THEREFORE, BE IT RESOLVED** that I, Dianne L. Watts, do hereby declare May 3, 2014 as "Surrey World Labyrinth Day" in the City of Surrey.

Mayor Dianne L. Watts
City of Surrey

92   Diana Ng

This book about labyrinths written in secular context welcomes all—whoever you are, wherever you are on this journey of life. The labyrinth is a valuable instrument for mindfulness and walking meditation, with many applications in both personal and professional spheres. Since the only constant in life is change, having skills to remain peaceful is quintessential as we navigate the transitions that life plans for us and the ones we make ourselves. When life challenges us with physical, emotional, and/or spiritual demands; when anger, hate, and other negative feelings accompany us; when circumstances are hopeless, full of angst, and confusing—the labyrinth brings us back to the present moments, makes us let go of yesterday, and urges us not to worry so much about tomorrow.

At times, when adversity arises, when our worldview becomes paradoxical and complicated—when it is difficult to choose when to let go and hold close; when to give and to receive; when to remain the same and when to make changes—the mindfulness act of paying attention, and being nonjudgmental in the present moment, may shift us to clarity and effectiveness. Life is precious and beautiful, truly a gift which we must treasure. Make the time and effort to live a life of well-being and perhaps the desire to live it again a second time.

To develop and maintain a discipline for mindfulness, and to explore walking meditation on the labyrinth, find a community you like and where you feel a sense of belonging. Group synergy sustains a meditative practice. Over time, an attitude for appreciating life and being well will develop. A deeper consciousness, a broader understanding, gives us "the serenity to accept the things we cannot change, the courage to change the things we can, and the wisdom to know the difference."

I encourage you to walk the labyrinth and discover its possibilities for yourself. However you choose to make sense of what happens in the labyrinth is yours to keep. Make the experience yours. Peace and possibilities assured. Enjoy!

*   *   *

*May you be filled with loving kindness.*

*May you be well.*

*May you be peaceful and at ease.*

*May you be happy.*

*May you be filled with loving kindness.*

*May you be well.*

*May you be peaceful and at ease.*

*May you be happy.*

—ANCIENT TIBETAN BUDDHIST BLESSING

# Directory of Labyrinths
# in Metro Vancouver

THE BEST RESOURCE FOR LOCATING LABYRINTHS THROUGH-
out the world is the website labyrinthlocator.com. Note that many
churches have portable labyrinths made of cloth, canvas, or vinyl,
which are taken out of storage for special occasions or public
events. Below is a partial list of permanent floor or ground labyrinths around Greater Vancouver.

Crossroads Hospice Society
Labyrinth type: Classical (Outdoor)
Pioneer Memorial Park, at the intersection of
Ioco Road and Heritage Mountain Boulevard, Port Moody, BC
604–469–4500
www.portmoody.ca/index.aspx?page=713

Fleetwood Park
Labyrinth type: Classical (Outdoor)
15802 – 80 Avenue, Surrey, BC
604–591–4011
www.surrey.ca

Forest Grove Elementary School
Labyrinth type: Classical (Outdoor)
8525 Forest Grove Drive, Burnaby, BC V5A 4H5
604–664–8690
forestgrove.sd41.bc.ca/

Historic Fenn Lodge
Labyrinth type: Classical (Outdoor)
Box 67, 15500 Morris Valley Road, Harrison Mills, BC VOM 1LO
604–796–9798 (toll free: 1–888–990–3399)
(No website)

Kwantlen Polytechnic University
Labyrinth type: Classical (Outdoor)
12666 – 72 Avenue, Surrey, BC V3W 2M8
604–599–2000
www.kpu.ca

Kwomais Point Park
Labyrinth type: Classical (Outdoor)
1367 – 128 Street, Surrey, BC
604–591–4011
www.surrey.ca

Ladner United Church
Labyrinth type: Classical (Indoor)
4960 – 48th Avenue, Delta, BC V4K 4X6
604–94–6254
www.ladnerunited.org

Mill Lake Park
Labyrinth type: Classical (Outdoor)
32960 Mill Lake Road, Abbotsford, BC
604–859–3134
www.abbotsford.ca

Sendall Gardens
Labyrinth type: Classical (Outdoor)
20166 – 50th Avenue, Langley, BC
604–514–2865
www.city.langley.bc.ca/

Shaughnessy Heights United Church
Labyrinth type: Chartres (Indoor)
1550 West 33rd Avenue, Vancouver, BC V6M 1A7
604–261–6377
shuc.ca/spirituality-worship/labyrinth

Simon Fraser University
Labyrinth type: Chartres (Outdoor)
8888 University Drive, Burnaby, BC V5A 1S6
778–782–3111
www.sfu.ca

St. Alban Anglican Church
Labyrinth type: Chartres (Outdoor)
7260 St Alban Road, Richmond , BC V6Y 2K3
604–278–2770
www.stalbansrichmond.org

St. John the Evangelist Anglican Church
Labyrinth type: Chartres (Outdoor)
220 West 8th Street, North Vancouver, BC V7M 1N1
604–986–1151
stjohnnv.ca/our-labyrinth/

St. Mary's Kerrisdale Church
Labyrinth type: Chartres (Indoor)
2490 West 37th Avenue, Vancouver, BC V6M 1P5
604–261–4228
stmaryskerrisdale.ca/main/about-us/labyrinth/

St. Paul's Anglican Church
Labyrinth type: Chartres (Indoor)
1130 Jervis Street, Vancouver, BC V6E 2C7
604–685–6832 #17
stpaulsanglican.bc.ca/#labyrinth

Vancouver School of Theology
Labyrinth type: Maltese Labyrinth (Outdoor)
6000 Iona Drive, Vancouver, BC V6T 1L4
604–822–9031
www.vst.edu/main/prospective-students/student-life/
spiritual-resources

Yewstone Gardens (Private)
Labyrinth type: Classical (Outdoor)
www.soulgardening.ca

# Resources

## A Wooden Finger Labyrinth for Individual Use in Home or Office

12½-inches diameter wooden finger labyrinth
A therapeutic tool that is perfect for home and office use.
It can also be used as an art piece.

**To purchase, visit labyrinthlady.ca/shop/**

· · ·

# A Personal–Size Floor Labyrinth
## for Use in Office or Home

Adorable 6- by 6-foot Classical three-circuit
floor labyrinth made of durable heavy canvas
Ideal for private moments.

**To purchase, visit labyrinthlady.ca/shop/**

. . .

# A Group-Size Floor Labyrinth

Attractive 19- by 19-foot Classical seven-circuit
floor labyrinth made of durable vinyl
An ancient tool with an enlarged center that is perfect
for individual use as well as for group activities.

**To purchase, visit labyrinthlady.ca/shop/**

# About the Author

 Diana Ng, R.N., B.SC.N., M.A., is a registered nurse with a master's degree in leadership; she worked for over twenty years in health promotions and postsecondary education. Currently, she is an award-winning speaker and consultant, encouraging openness, equality, and collaborative leadership in organizations. She is recognized by her community as the Labyrinth Lady.

**Need to enhance morale or develop interpersonal relations in your organization? Looking for a motivational speaker or professional workshop leader?**

**Call (+1) 604–765–7493 or email diana@labyrinthlady.ca to book your next appointment**

**Visit her website: www.labyrinthlady.ca**

**You can also connect with Diana on social media:**

www.facebook.com/vancouverlabyrinth

twitter.com/diana_ng

www.linkedin.com/in/ngdiana

plus.google.com/+DianaNglabyrinth

www.pinterest.com/vanlabyrinth

instagram.com/vancouverlabyrinth

www.youtube.com/channel/UCXvM5jbQzJ79reUa-lej7Ew

# Coming Soon

A FORTHCOMING BOOK BY
DIANA NG, R.N., B.SC.N., M.A. LEADERSHIP

*Walking the Labyrinth: An Uncommon Path to Leadership*